Lecture Notes
in Business Information Processing 561

Series Editors

Wil van der Aalst⬤, *RWTH Aachen University, Aachen, Germany*
Sudha Ram⬤, *University of Arizona, Tucson, USA*
Michael Rosemann⬤, *Queensland University of Technology, Brisbane, Australia*
Clemens Szyperski, *Microsoft Research, Redmond, USA*
Giancarlo Guizzardi⬤, *University of Twente, Enschede, The Netherlands*

LNBIP reports state-of-the-art results in areas related to business information systems and industrial application software development – timely, at a high level, and in both printed and electronic form.

The type of material published includes

- Proceedings (published in time for the respective event)
- Postproceedings (consisting of thoroughly revised and/or extended final papers)
- Other edited monographs (such as, for example, project reports or invited volumes)
- Tutorials (coherently integrated collections of lectures given at advanced courses, seminars, schools, etc.)
- Award-winning or exceptional theses

LNBIP is abstracted/indexed in DBLP, EI and Scopus. LNBIP volumes are also submitted for the inclusion in ISI Proceedings.

Sibylle Peter · Martin Kropp · Torgeir Dingsøyr ·
Clare Dillon · Philipp Diebold · Deepti Jain ·
Maria Ilaria Lunesu · Andrea Pinna
Editors

Agile Processes in Software Engineering and Extreme Programming – Workshops

XP 2025 Workshops
Brugg-Windisch, Switzerland, June 2–5, 2025
Revised Selected Papers

Editors
Sibylle Peter
University of Applied Sciences and Arts
Northwestern Switzerland
Windisch, Switzerland

Martin Kropp
University of Applied Sciences and Arts
Northwestern Switzerland
Windisch, Switzerland

Torgeir Dingsøyr
NTNU and SimulaMet
Trondheim, Norway

Clare Dillon
University of Galway
Galway, Ireland

Philipp Diebold
IU International University of Applied
Science and Bagilstein GmbH
Erfurt, Germany

Deepti Jain
AgileVirgin
Gurgaon Haryana, Delhi, India

Andrea Pinna
University of Cagliari
Cagliari, Italy

Maria Ilaria Lunesu
University of Cagliari
Cagliari, Italy

ISSN 1865-1348 ISSN 1865-1356 (electronic)
Lecture Notes in Business Information Processing
ISBN 978-3-032-05798-3 ISBN 978-3-032-05799-0 (eBook)
https://doi.org/10.1007/978-3-032-05799-0

© The Editor(s) (if applicable) and The Author(s) 2026. This book is an open access publication.

Open Access This book is licensed under the terms of the Creative Commons Attribution 4.0 International License (http://creativecommons.org/licenses/by/4.0/), which permits use, sharing, adaptation, distribution and reproduction in any medium or format, as long as you give appropriate credit to the original author(s) and the source, provide a link to the Creative Commons license and indicate if changes were made.
The images or other third party material in this book are included in the book's Creative Commons license, unless indicated otherwise in a credit line to the material. If material is not included in the book's Creative Commons license and your intended use is not permitted by statutory regulation or exceeds the permitted use, you will need to obtain permission directly from the copyright holder.
The use of general descriptive names, registered names, trademarks, service marks, etc. in this publication does not imply, even in the absence of a specific statement, that such names are exempt from the relevant protective laws and regulations and therefore free for general use.
The publisher, the authors and the editors are safe to assume that the advice and information in this book are believed to be true and accurate at the date of publication. Neither the publisher nor the authors or the editors give a warranty, expressed or implied, with respect to the material contained herein or for any errors or omissions that may have been made. The publisher remains neutral with regard to jurisdictional claims in published maps and institutional affiliations.

This Springer imprint is published by the registered company Springer Nature Switzerland AG
The registered company address is: Gewerbestrasse 11, 6330 Cham, Switzerland

If disposing of this product, please recycle the paper.

Preface

With great pleasure we introduce this volume of research proceeding from the material of the research workshops and the posters track of the 26th International Conference on Agile Software Development, XP 2025, held during June 2-5, 2025, at the University of Applied Sciences and Arts Northwestern Switzerland in Brugg-Windisch, Switzerland.

Research papers from the XP 2025 conference were published in the conference proceedings, LNBIP volume 545. This companion volume, published after the conference, contains selected revised papers from two workshops and from the poster tracks, and includes revised summaries of three workshops.

The main ambition with the workshops was to foster collaboration, generate new insights, and advance the field of agile software development. In all, we received ten proposals for research workshops, of which six were accepted. We sought to select workshops with a high degree of interactivity, which could attract 15-40 participants the day before the main conference. Two workshops were unfortunately cancelled, one as the proposal was withdrawn and another due to a lack of paper submissions.

The research workshop program consisted of two full-day and two half-day workshops. The four workshops gathered interest from 14-34 participants, and the summaries show insights generated in the sessions:

- Agile Enterprise Architecture and Delivery
- AI and Agile Software Development: From Frustration to Success
- The Third International Workshop on Global and Hybrid Work in Software Engineering (GoHyb)
- Towards a closer collaboration between practice and research in Agile Software Development – What we learnt; and what not?

The research poster track culminated with an exhibition held on June 4 and included 6 posters, out of which 3 were accepted for publication.

The number of submitted research papers to workshops and poster tracks was 35, out of which 9 were accepted for publication in these post-proceedings. The review cycles used single-blind reviews in EasyChair.

A call for papers for the workshops and a call for participation were published on the SEWORLD mailing list. For the first time, conference participants could indicate interest in workshops when registering.

We extend our sincere thanks to the authors whose work is featured in this volume for advancing the discourse in agile software development. We would like to thank the workshop organisers for all their efforts in fostering collaboration and advancing the field of agile software development. Our gratitude also goes to the reviewers for their dedication and thoughtful feedback, which ensured the high quality of these papers. We also acknowledge the significant contributions of all speakers, sponsors, shepherds, chairs, and volunteers who helped bring this conference to life. Special thanks are extended to the XP Conference Steering Committee and the sponsor, "the School of Computer Science of the University of Applied Sciences and Arts Northwestern Switzerland".

June 2025

Martin Kropp
Sibylle Peter
Clare Dillon
Torgeir Dingsøyr
Philipp Diebold
Deepti Jain
Maria Ilaria Lunesu
Andrea Pinna

Organization

Conference Co-chairs

Sibylle Peter — University of Applied Sciences and Arts Northwestern Switzerland

Martin Kropp — University of Applied Sciences and Arts Northwestern Switzerland

Workshops Co-chairs

Clare Dillon — University of Galway, Ireland
Torgeir Dingsøyr — Norwegian University of Science and Technology and SimulaMET, Norway

Posters Track Co-chairs

Philipp Diebold — IU International University of Applied Science, Germany
Deepti Jain — AgileVirgin, India

Publication Co-chairs

Andrea Pinna — University of Cagliari, Italy
Maria Ilaria Lunesu — University of Cagliari, Italy

Workshops Organizers

Agile Enterprise Architecture and Delivery

Nora Sleumer — Swiss Informatics Society, Switzerland
Simon Moser — SolutionBoxX Ltd, Switzerland

AI and Agile Software Development: From Frustration to Success

Pekka Abrahamsson	Tampere University, Finland
Tomas Herda	Austrian Post Group IT, Austria
Victoria Pichler	Austrian Post Group IT, Austria
Geir Kjetil Hanssen	SINTEF, Norway
Alex Polyakov	ProjectSimple.ai, USA
Zheying Zhang	Tampere University, Finland

Third International Workshop on Global and Hybrid Work in Software Engineering (GoHyb)

Maria Paasivaara	LUT University, Finland and Aalto University, Finland
Dron Khanna	Free University of Bozen-Bolzano, Italy
Sonja Hyrynsalmi	LUT University, Finland

Towards a closer collaboration between practice and research in Agile Software Development – What we learnt; and what not?

Michael Neumann	University of Applied Sciences & Arts Hannover, Germany
Eva-Maria Schön	University of Applied Sciences Emden/Leer, Germany
Maria Rauschenberger	University of Applied Sciences Emden/Leer, Germany
Mali Senapathi	Auckland University of Technology, New Zealand
Tiago Silva da Silva	Federal University of São Paulo, Brazil

Program Committee

Alex Polyakov	ProjectSimple.ai, USA
Anastasiia Tkalich	SINTEF, Norway
Anh Nguyen Duc	University of South Eastern Norway, Norway
Aurora Vizcaíno	Universidad de Castilla - La Mancha, Spain
Bettina Scherb	UK
Casper Lassenius	Aalto University, Finland and Simula Metropolitan Center for Digital Engineering, Norway
Christof Ebert	Vector Consulting, Germany

Edona Elshan	Vrije Universiteit Amsterdam, Netherlands
Filippo Lanubile	University of Bari, Italy
Helen Sharp	Open University, UK
Iflaah Salman	Lappeenranta-Lahti University of Technology, Finland
Jorge Melegati	Free University of Bozen-Bolzano, Italy
Kai-Kristian Kemell	Tampere University, Finland
Karl Josef Gstettner	AMS Austria
Martin Eder	Austrian Post Group IT, Austria
Mika Saari	Tampere University, Finland
Ricardo Britto	Ericsson/Blekinge Institute of Technology, Sweden
Ronnie de Souza Santos	University of Calgary, Canada
The Anh Nguyen	CREST, University of Adelaide, Australia
Tor Sporsem	SINTEF, Norway
Viggo Tellefsen Wivestad	SINTEF, Norway
Viktoria Stray	University of Oslo/SINTEF, Norway
Yuliia Pieskova	Alpha Affinity, Germany

Steering Committee

Peggy Gregory (chair)	University of Glasgow, UK
Hubert Baumeister	Technical University of Denmark, Denmark
François Coallier	École de Technologie Supérieure, Canada
Jutta Eckstein	Independent, Germany
Hendrik Esser	Ericsson, Germany
Juan Garbajosa	Universidad Politécnica de Madrid, Spain
Martin Kropp	University of Applied Sciences and Arts Northwestern Switzerland, Switzerland
Wouter Lagerweij	Lagerweij Consultancy, Netherlands
Maria Paasivaara	LUT University & Aalto University, Norway
Viktoria Stray	University of Oslo, Norway
Xiaofeng Wang	Free University of Bozen-Bolzano, Italy

Sponsoring Organization

School of Computer Science of University of Applied Sciences and Arts Northwestern Switzerland, Switzerland

Contents

AI and Agile Software Development: From Frustration to Success

AI and Agile Software Development: From Frustration to Success XP2025 Workshop Summary 3
   Tomas Herda, Victoria Pichler, Zheying Zhang, Pekka Abrahamsson, and Geir K. Hanssen

From Constraints to Capabilities: AI as a Force Multiplier 14
   Evan Leybourn and Christopher Morales

Why Adapt RAG for Agile? Challenges, Frameworks, and the Role of Evaluator Agent 22
   Ayman Asad Khan, Md Toufique Hasan, Mika Saari, Kai-Kristian Kemell, and Jussi Rasku

AI and Teamwork in Agile Software Development: A Systematic Mapping Study 32
   Ya Ting Crystal Kwok and Mahum Adil

NLP and GenAI in Agile Project Management: A Systematic Mapping Study 41
   Daniel Planötscher

The Third International Workshop on Global and Hybrid Work in Software Engineering (GoHyb)

Hybrid Work in Agile Software Engineering: Current Research and Future Directions 53
   Fateme Broomandi, Maria Paasivaara, Emily Laue Christensen, Sonja Hyrynsalmi, and Dron Khanna

Are there any Differences in the Way that Software Engineers Perceive their Productivity Depending on their Work Style? 68
   Gabriela Aranda, Aurora Vizcaíno, Juan Pablo Soto, Elvira Rolón, Kelly Garcés, and Félix O. García

Understanding Factors Influencing Trust in Software Development Teams in Hybrid Work Settings: An Empirical Investigation 78
   Sulabh Tyagi and Zainab Masood

Towards a closer collaboration between practice and research in Agile Software Development – What we learnt; and what not?

Towards a Closer Collaboration Between Practice and Research in Agile Software Development Workshop: A Summary and Research Agenda 91
   Michael Neumann, Eva-Maria Schön, Mali Senapathi, Maria Rauschenberger, and Tiago Silva da Silva

Posters Track

Lessons from a Big-Bang Integration: Challenges in Edge Computing and Machine Learning 101
   Alessandro Aneggi and Andrea Janes

Novice Programmers' Experiences with Hybrid vs. In-Person Pair Programming – A Comparative Study 108
   Mary Giblin and Sheila Fallon

Rethink Agile Scaling with Robotics Subsumption Architecture 114
   Sue Ryu

Author Index 121

AI and Agile Software Development: From Frustration to Success

AI and Agile Software Development: From Frustration to Success XP2025 Workshop Summary

Tomas Herda[1](✉) [iD], Victoria Pichler[2] [iD], Zheying Zhang[3] [iD],
Pekka Abrahamsson[3] [iD], and Geir K. Hanssen[4] [iD]

[1] AI Center of Excellence - Austrian Post, Vienna, Austria
herda.tom@gmail.com
[2] Digital Logistics Platform - Group-IT - Austrian Post, Vienna, Austria
[3] Tampere University, Tampere, Finland
[4] SINTEF, 7034 Trondheim, Norway

Abstract. The full-day workshop on AI and Agile at XP 2025 convened a diverse group of researchers and industry practitioners to address the practical challenges and opportunities of integrating Artificial Intelligence into Agile software development. Through interactive sessions, participants identified shared frustrations related to integrating AI into Agile Software Development practices, including challenges with tooling, governance, data quality, and critical skill gaps. These challenges were systematically prioritized and analyzed to uncover root causes. The workshop culminated in the collaborative development of a research roadmap that pinpoints actionable directions for future work, including both immediate solutions and ambitious long-term goals. The key outcome is a structured agenda designed to foster joint industry-academic efforts to move from identified frustrations to successful implementation.

Keywords: Artificial Intelligence · AI and Agile · Agile Software Development · Research Roadmap · Human-AI Collaboration · Prompt Engineering · AI Governance · Software Engineering · Workshop Report

1 Workshop Overview

The "AI and Agile Software Development: From Frustration to Success" workshop at XP 2025 brought together a diverse group of researchers and industry practitioners. The event was designed to move beyond theoretical discussions and address the practical realities of integrating Artificial Intelligence into Agile software development. While numerous studies such as [1–5] have explored the use of AI in Agile contexts, industrial experience and practitioner feedback remain underrepresented yet essential to grounding and advancing this research. To bridge this gap, the workshop deliberately invited contributions from both academia and industry. It marked the third consecutive year of a dedicated AI and Agile event at the XP Conference, building on the foundations of previous workshops at XP2023 and also AI and Agile Industry and Practice Track at XP2024[1]. The significant interest in the topic was clear from the 17 total submissions received, from which two keynotes, three peer-reviewed research papers, and three industrial experience talks were accepted for presentation. The workshop successfully brought together a diverse group of 35 industrial practitioners and researchers.

The workshop had four primary goals:

- To explore the intersection of AI and Agile methodologies.
- To share real-world experiences, including both challenges and successes.
- To collaboratively build future research pathways for the industry.
- To use AI tools for preparation, participant support, and post-event access.

The organizing committee represented a balanced academic-industrial consortium, comprising practitioners from Austrian Post and researchers from Tampere University and SINTEF. The workshop format guided participants from sharing individual experiences toward a collective understanding, culminating the co-creation of a research roadmap.

A noteworthy innovation was the deliberate integration of AI-generated outputs to document and extend the workshop activities. This resulted in several digital artifacts designed to capture and share the event's outcomes. An AI-generated song captured the collaborative spirit, while a custom GPT was developed to serve as a persistent, interactive knowledge base for anyone interested in the workshop's content. These resources[2], along with video recordings and the official program and workshop website, provide a comprehensive and lasting record of the discussions.

To demonstrate the practical application of the workshop's themes, the organizers used a variety of AI tools throughout the entire workshop lifecycle.

- **Creative Content & Preparation:** The official workshop theme song was generated by **Suno.com** using custom instructions, with lyrics written by the **GPT-o4-mini** model. The presentation slides used throughout the day were created with the **Gamma.app AI Tool**, featuring images generated by the **Flux Fast 1.1** model.
- **Data Processing & Analysis:** After the retrospective session, handwritten notes on flipcharts were transcribed using the **Gemma 3 27B** model. The collected frustrations were then systematically grouped and categorized with the help of the **GPT-4o** model.

---

[1] XP2024AI and Agile - Industry and Practice Track.
[2] Final Workshop Program: https://conf.researchr.org/home/xp-2025/aiandagile-2025
Official Workshop Website: gpt-lab.eu
Custom Conference GPT: chatgpt.com
AI-Generated Workshop Song: suno.com
Workshop Opening Talk: https://youtu.be/xigzwCzttV4 Workshop Highlights Video: https://www.youtube.com/watch?v=TmQwxuRAOIk.

– **Reporting & Knowledge Sharing:** An initial draft of this workshop summary was created with assistance from the **Gemini 2.5 Pro** model. Furthermore, the **AIAndAgileXP2025GPT**, a custom knowledge base, was created using OpenAI's platform. It runs on the **GPT-4o** model and was given custom instructions to "Act as a friendly, knowledgeable assistant..." along with access to all accepted papers, keynotes, and this summary, creating a lasting knowledge base accessible to anyone long after the workshop has concluded.

The remainder of this summary follows the chronological structure of the workshop agenda. Section 2 describes the opening networking activities and keynote presentations that framed the day. Section 3 captures the retrospective session, where participants articulated frustrations, successes, and key lessons from AI integration in Agile contexts. Section 4 presents the review and ideation talks, highlighting current practices and future directions. Section 5 synthesizes the collaborative research roadmap developed during the final session. The summary concludes in Sect. 6 with a call to action and the proposal for a Living Lab format to continue advancing this emerging research-practice agenda.

2 Setting the Stage: Networking and Keynotes

The day began with a facilitated networking session designed to connect peers and establish a collaborative atmosphere. The session was structured in two rounds to encourage both practical and creative engagement. In the first round, "Experience Sharing," participants were asked: "What's one specific challenge or success you've seen when integrating AI into Agile workflows? How did you overcome the challenge or how did you succeed?" This question immediately grounded the workshop in practical experience. The second round, "Creative Reflection," shifted the tone by asking: "'If I Were an AI...' what would your Superpower be?" This activity fostered a more imaginative mindset and built rapport among attendees before the deeper technical sessions.

Two keynotes provided foundational perspectives that framed the day's discussions and offered diverse viewpoints on the interplay between AI technologies and Agile practices.

Keynote 1: eXtreme Programming with Artificial Intelligence by Joshua Kerievsky

Joshua Kerievsky explored the relationship between AI and eXtreme Programming (XP). He argued that to craft excellent software with AI, teams get better results by following XP's core values and practices. The talk focused on how and when XP principles help produce successful outcomes in a human-AI collaborative model. The key takeaway was that established software engineering disciplines are not obsolete in the age of AI. Instead, they provide the necessary structure and quality control to effectively guide and validate AI-generated outputs.

Keynote 2: Lessons Learned Building an AI Driven Project Management Platform by Alex Polyakov

Alex Polyakov discussed the development of ProjectSimple.ai, an AI-powered project management platform built to tackle common challenges like misaligned goals, fragmented data, and unclear project status. He introduced a four-domain model 'Behavioral, Systematic, Analytical, Adaptive' to highlight where AI can meaningfully support Agile workflows. Rather than replicating Agile frameworks, he emphasized that tools should address real team issues and provide insights that improve decision making, clarity, and adaptability. Ultimately, it is the ability to influence the right behaviors that makes the real difference.

3 Uncovering Collective Experience: The Retrospective Session

The first major interactive component of the workshop was a retrospective session designed to gather empirical insights from participants' experiences with AI integration in Agile software development. Through structured small-group discussions, attendees explored three thematic areas, and they are frustrations, successes, and lessons learned. Following the small-group discussions, a Gallery Walk facilitation technique was used. This allowed all participants to circulate and review the key findings documented at each table, ensuring a shared understanding of the collective insights before the synthesis. This process revealed a remarkable consistency in the challenges, successes, and lessons learned by practitioners and researchers alike.

Shared Frustrations

The first round focused on challenges, asking participants *"What has been your biggest frustration when trying to integrate AI into your Agile workflows?"*. The frustrations identified by the groups clustered around three key themes.

Tooling and Model Behavior: A primary source of frustration was the tooling itself. Participants noted there were *"too many tools"* to choose from, making selection difficult. They also cited a *"lack of temperature controls on LLM UI"* and the problem of being *"forced to use MS Copilot."* The rapid pace of change in models was a challenge, as were *"slow local language models."* A significant pain point was the unreliability of AI outputs, with participants mentioning *"hallucinations,"* *"making same mistakes again even after fixing before,"* and getting *"non-deterministic answers."*

Data, Privacy, and Governance: Data was a major concern. Issues included *"poor data quality,"* the difficulty of controlling privacy, and a lack of clarity around *"regulation compliance."* A specific and potent frustration was the opaqueness of data usage policies, captured by the statement: *"We don't know what's behind the checkbox"* when opting out of data collection for model training.

Human and Process Factors: Integrating AI into teams and workflows presented its own set of problems. Participants observed an *"over-reliance on AI for junior developers"* and *"poor architectural choices by AI."* A critical frustration was the feeling that the *"invested time"* did not always lead to *"valuable outcomes."* Teams also struggled with the *"early give up"* phenomenon when initial experiments with AI tools did not succeed.

Celebrated Successes

Despite the frustrations, participants shared many positive outcomes. The second round shifted to positive outcomes, with the guiding question: *"Where have you seen AI add real value in Agile practices, including successful use cases, impactful tools, or innovative approaches where AI has enhanced productivity or team collaboration?"* In response to the question, participants identified the following contributions.

Productivity and Acceleration: AI was widely successful in accelerating tasks. Examples included *"quick proof of concept (PoC) for software startup," "headstart for code,"* and *"unit test generation."* It was also valuable for *"writing user stories & acceptance tests"* and *"workshop preparation."* The sentiment of *"never having to start from a blank page again"* was a powerful, recurring theme.

Content and Code Generation: The most cited successes involved content creation. This included *"code generation & debugging," "code documentation," "creative writing,"* and using AI as a *"personal writing coach."*

Expanding Capabilities: AI was seen as a way to blend role boundaries and help individuals perform tasks outside their core expertise, such as *"help with marketing"* or *"social media marketing."* It also served as a tool for discovery, helping users *"discover new features"* or act as an *"AI strategy advisor."*

Key Lessons Learned

The final round synthesized these experiences, prompting discussion with: *"What key lessons have you learned from using AI in Agile environments? What would you repeat, avoid, or do differently next time?"* The lessons learned reflected a growing maturity in how teams approach AI.

Human Oversight is Critical: A dominant lesson was that human judgment remains essential. Phrases like *"review generated code critically," "the human factor is becoming important,"* and *"don't trust AI, review output"* were common. The goal is an *"embracing human-AI relationship,"* not replacement.

Skills and Literacy are Foundational: Participants concluded that *"AI literacy is key"* and *"prompting is essential."* The insight that *"writing prompts is similar to writing code"* suggests a need for a more disciplined approach to interacting with AI.

Strategic Tool Use is Necessary: Instead of relying on a single tool, a key lesson was to *"use more AI tools"* and *"cross-check different models."* Participants found it helpful to *"develop your own GPT"* for specific tasks and understand which tool is an *"expert"* at which outputs.

4 Sharing Current Practices: The Review and Ideation Session

This session featured a series of short presentations from both academic and industry contributors. The presentations were divided into two parts: "Review," which focused on current applications, and "Ideation," which explored future visions. It is important to note that only the three accepted research papers will be included in the official conference proceedings.

Review Presentations

The review talks highlighted practical frameworks for applying AI to specific Agile challenges.

- Ayman Asad Khan's presentation, "Why Adapt RAG for Agile? Challenges, Frameworks, and the Role of Evaluator Agent" explored the challenges of using Retrieval-Augmented Generation in Agile contexts and proposed a framework that includes an "Evaluator Agent" to improve output quality.
- Daniel Planötscher discussed "AI-driven requirements gathering" showing how AI can assist in one of the earliest and most critical phases of the software development lifecycle.

Ideation Presentations

The ideation talks looked toward the future, raising important questions and presenting new research.

- Dorota Mleczko asked, "Where Are All the Agile Leaders in the AI Revolution?" pointing to a need for stronger leadership to guide AI adoption in Agile organizations.
- Crystal Kwok presented "AI and Teamwork in Agile Software Development: A Systematic Mapping Study" analyzing existing research on how AI impacts team dynamics.
- Evan Leybourn and Chris Morales spoke on "From Constraints to Capabilities: AI as a Force Multiplier" framing AI as a force multiplier that can transform team potential.
- Daniel Planötscher presented "NLP and GenAI in Agile Project Management: A Systematic Mapping Study" offering a comprehensive overview of research in that area.

These presentations provided concrete examples and forward-thinking concepts that fueled the subsequent roadmap discussion.

5 Building the Future: The Research Roadmap Session

This final, highly interactive session was the culmination of the day's work. The objective was to synthesize the collected insights into a collaborative research roadmap.

F1: Tooling Challenges - Tooling immaturity (15 total votes)
- **Too many tools, unclear which to use – 73.3%**
- Limited model controls (temperature, context window) – 13.3%
- Forced or constrained tool usage (e.g., MS Copilot) – 13.3%
- Model behavior changes too frequently – 0.0%

F2. Governance & Compliance (15 total votes)
- **Unclear data privacy and protection boundaries – 53.3%**
- Lack of transparency in model decisions – 33.3%
- Uncertainty about regulation and compliance – 13.3%

F3. Team & Process Misalignment (17 total votes)
- **AI integration doesn't yield valuable outcomes – 52.9%**
- AI used poorly in learning and team settings – 23.5%
- Poor design decisions suggested by AI – 17.6%
- Over-reliance on AI in junior roles – 5.9%

F4. Data & Model Quality Issues (18 total votes)
- **Hallucinations and unreliable outputs — 66.7%**
- Hard to assess AI answer quality — 22.2%
- Poor or inconsistent data quality — 5.6%
- Responses too verbose or irrelevant — 5.6%

F5. Knowledge & Prompting Gaps (14 total votes)
- **Lack of prompting skills or best practices – 78.6%**
- Missing or insufficient context in prompts – 14.3%
- Repeated model errors despite fixes – 7.1%

F6. Creativity (8 total votes)
- **AI lacks creativity and originality – 75%**
- Multimodality – 25%

Fig. 1. Voting Results from Participants Across Six Frustration Categories

Prioritizing Challenges

The session began by presenting the six major frustration categories that were synthesized by an AI from the notes in the retrospective session. These categories, including tooling challenges, governance and compliance, team and process misalignment, data quality issues, knowledge gaps, and creativity limitations, provided a scaffold for focused discussion.

To prioritize areas of concern, participants voted on the most pressing sub-challenges within each category using a collaborative Padlet board [6]. This data-driven approach ensured the subsequent deep dive focused on the issues the group collectively deemed most important.

Figure 1 summarizes the voting results from all six frustration categories prioritized by the workshop participants. The top concerns included too many tools and lack of clarity on which to use (F1), unclear data privacy and protection boundaries (F2), AI integration that doesn't yield valuable outcomes (F3), hallucinations and unreliable outputs (F4), lack of prompting skills or best practices (F5), and lack of creativity and originality in AI outputs (F6).

Collaborative Deep Dive

Participants broke into three groups, each tackling two of the prioritized frustration areas. Their task was to identify root causes, knowledge gaps, and propose both actionable short-term actions, i.e. low-hanging fruit and ambitious long-term goals i.e. moonshot ideas.

Group 1: Tooling Challenges (F1) and Creativity Limitations (F6)

- **Root Causes:** This group identified *"capitalism baked in 'new' tools"* as a driver for the overwhelming number of options. For the lack of creativity, they pointed to the inherent nature of models trained on existing data.
- **Knowledge & Research Gaps:** A key gap identified was the lack of trust in AI tools and a need to better understand how to write effective prompts to elicit more creative or useful responses.
- **Low-Hanging Fruit:** The group proposed creating a *"shared document on which tool to use for what objective"* as a practical, cross-industry resource. They also suggested focusing on the *"human-AI partnership for creative use cases."*
- **Moonshot Idea:** Their ambitious idea was a *"UI that taps into multiple tools/agents that chooses the best model"* for a given task, potentially augmented with the *"thought process of people that have made successful products."*
- **Future Research:** Research should focus on *"how to write better prompts for tools"* to improve both utility and creativity.

Group 2: Governance (F2) and Knowledge Gaps (F5)

- **Root Causes:** Unclear privacy boundaries and a lack of prompting skills were traced back to a need for more transparency, better knowledge transfer, and more effective training.
- **Knowledge & Research Gaps:** The group highlighted a need for more trust in AI, which can only be built with better data privacy, security, and specialized agents for specific tasks.
- **Low-Hanging Fruit:** For governance, they suggested using a *"closed system, small model for testing"* to better understand AI's impact in a safe environment. To address the skills gap, they proposed a *"commitment to training"* and developing a *"coworker culture with AI."*
- **Moonshot Idea:** The governance moonshot was to *"create your own LLM"* for full control. For the skills gap, they envisioned *"shadow agents"* running on projects in parallel to provide comparative analysis and recommendations.

- **Future Research:** Research is needed on creating safe, secure environments for AI use (e.g., recording meetings) and on the effectiveness of different training methods for AI literacy.

Group 3: Process Misalignment (F3) and Data Quality (F4)

 - **Root Causes:** The group identified *"missing AI literacy"* as the primary root cause for both AI integrations failing to provide value and for teams being unable to handle hallucinations. Other causes included unclear success criteria, poor data quality, and the *"fear of investing in multiple LLMs."*
 - **Knowledge & Research Gaps:** There is a significant gap in understanding the *"quantitative business benefits of AI."* Teams also lack effective strategies for validating AI output and need better *"multi-LLM solutions."*
 - **Low-Hanging Fruit:** A practical first step is for teams to clearly define success criteria and goals before implementing an AI solution.
 - **Moonshot Idea:** The group's moonshot was to develop a system that could robustly quantify the ROI of AI integration and provide a feedback loop to fine-tune solutions.
 - **Future Research:** Future research should focus on the *"quantitative business benefits of AI,"* the *"quantity and quality of AI training"* needed for teams, and the *"mindsets"* that are most effective for working with AI and avoiding early abandonment of the technology.

6 Conclusion and Call to Action

The workshop successfully created a much-needed space for open dialogue, bridging the gap between academic theory and industry practice. The most significant outcome was the clear alignment on the core frustrations and knowledge gaps shared by both communities. The challenges of tooling, governance, data quality, and skills are not unique to one domain; they are universal hurdles on the path to integrating AI effectively into Agile workflows. This resonance with recent studies [7–11] indicates the widespread nature of these challenges. The day's journey, from sharing individual frustrations to collaboratively building a research roadmap, demonstrated a powerful model for progress.

However, a roadmap is only a guide. To ensure the momentum from this workshop translates into tangible progress, we must move from discussion to action. The workshop identified that a primary reason "AI integration doesn't yield valuable outcomes" is a fundamental gap between knowing about AI and knowing how to use it effectively in a given context. Simply encouraging experimentation is not enough.

Therefore, we issue a specific call to action: **to launch the "AI and Agile Living Lab" as an interactive session at the future conference.**

This will not be a traditional track of presentations. Instead, it will be a structured, hands-on problem-solving environment designed to kickstart a continuous

"Learning Loop" for participants and their organizations. Drawing inspiration from proven methods for accelerating AI adoption, the Living Lab will operate on a simple but powerful principle: people learn best by applying AI to their own real work.

The proposed structure for the **AI and Agile Living Lab** is as follows:

1. **Bring Your Own Problem (BYOP):** Participants will come to the session with a genuine, unresolved challenge from their work at the intersection of AI and Agile. This could be a practitioner's struggle with generating test cases or a researcher's difficulty in analyzing qualitative data.
2. **Collaborative Work in Mixed Pairs:** Participants will be paired up, intentionally mixing industry practitioners with academic researchers. This structure fosters direct collaboration and knowledge exchange.
3. **Structured, Multi-Model Experimentation:** The lab will guide pairs to use several different AI models (e.g., GPT, Claude, Gemini) on their problem, comparing outputs and learning the unique strengths of each. This directly addresses the *"too many tools, unclear which to use"* frustration.
4. **Guided Prompting Techniques:** Participants will be introduced to and use structured prompting methods, moving beyond simple requests to craft effective, context-rich instructions for the AI. This directly tackles the top-voted frustration: *"lack of prompting skills or best practices."*
5. **Focus on Tangible Outcomes and Reflection:** The goal is not just to try, but to achieve. By the end of the session, each pair will aim to have a tangible output: a working code snippet, a set of refined user stories, a draft experimental design, or a new, documented workflow. The session will conclude with pairs sharing what they built, what they learned, and the *"moment of insight"* that made AI's value concrete for them.

By creating this Living Lab, we move beyond discussing the research roadmap and begin actively executing it. This format provides a direct, evidence-based response to the core challenges identified in our workshop. It builds the critical AI literacy our community needs, demonstrates tangible ROI on a personal scale, and forges the authentic practitioner-researcher collaborations required to solve our field's most pressing problems. We invite the entire community to join us in 2026, not just to talk about the future, but to build it together, one solved problem at a time.

References

1. Cinkusz, K., Chudziak, J.A.: Towards LLM-augmented multiagent systems for agile software engineering. In: Proceedings of the 39th IEEE/ACM International Conference on Automated Software Engineering, pp. 2476–2477 (2024)
2. Bahi, A., GHari, J., Gahi, Y.: Integrating generative AI for advancing agile software development and mitigating project management challenges. Int. J. Adv. Comput. Sci. Appl. **15**(3) (2024)

3. Zhang, Z., Rayhan, M., Herda, T., Goisauf, M., Abrahamsson, P.: LLM-based agents for automating the enhancement of user story quality: an early report. In: International Conference on Agile Software Development, pp. 117–126. Springer, Cham (2024)
4. Manish, S.: An autonomous multi-agent LLM framework for agile software development. Int. J. Trend Sci. Res. Dev. **8**(5), 892–898 (2024)
5. Cabrero-Daniel, B., Herda, T., Pichler, V., Eder, M.: Exploring human-AI collaboration in agile: customised LLM meeting assistants. In: International Conference on Agile Software Development, pp. 163–178. Springer, Cham (2024)
6. Xp2025: Aiandagile workshop: Developing research roadmap. https://padlet.com/embed/hsxlg0sr4k1235rd. Accessed 11 June 2025
7. Amershi, S., et al.: Guidelines for human-AI interaction. In: Proceedings of the 2019 CHI Conference on Human Factors in Computing Systems, pp. 1–13 (2019)
8. Ji, Z., et al.: Survey of hallucination in natural language generation. ACM Comput. Surv. **55**(12), 1–38 (2023)
9. Kulkarni, R.H., Padmanabham, P.: Integration of artificial intelligence activities in software development processes and measuring effectiveness of integration. IET Softw. **11**(1), 18–26 (2017)
10. Liu, P., Yuan, W., Fu, J., Jiang, Z., Hayashi, H., Neubig, G.: Pre-train, prompt, and predict: a systematic survey of prompting methods in natural language processing. ACM Comput. Surv. **55**(9), 1–35 (2023)
11. Shneiderman, B.: Human-centered artificial intelligence: reliable, safe & trustworthy. Int. J. Hum.-Comput. Interact. **36**(6), 495–504 (2020)

Open Access This chapter is licensed under the terms of the Creative Commons Attribution 4.0 International License (http://creativecommons.org/licenses/by/4.0/), which permits use, sharing, adaptation, distribution and reproduction in any medium or format, as long as you give appropriate credit to the original author(s) and the source, provide a link to the Creative Commons license and indicate if changes were made.

The images or other third party material in this chapter are included in the chapter's Creative Commons license, unless indicated otherwise in a credit line to the material. If material is not included in the chapter's Creative Commons license and your intended use is not permitted by statutory regulation or exceeds the permitted use, you will need to obtain permission directly from the copyright holder.

From Constraints to Capabilities: AI as a Force Multiplier

Evan Leybourn[✉] [iD] and Christopher Morales [iD]

Business Agility Institute, 76 Woodhill, Irvine, CA 92620, USA
{eleybourn,cmorales}@businessagility.institute

Abstract. This study explores the transformative potential of artificial intelligence (AI) as a force multiplier in modern organizations. Using the Delphi research method, a panel of experts across multiple industries assessed how AI can augment human capabilities, drive innovation, and unlock measurable business outcomes. The findings highlight a gap between AI's promise and the actual benefits realized, often due to organizational constraints such as rigid budgeting, poor data quality, and low workforce readiness. To fully leverage AI, organizations must shift their focus to human-centric business capabilities, including dynamic funding, agile workflows, and continuous learning. This paper presents practical guidance for overcoming constraints and enabling a more adaptive, capability-driven approach to AI adoption.

Keywords: Artificial Intelligence · Business Agility · Organizational Design · Force Multiplier · AI Adoption · Decision-Making · Capability Development

1 Introduction

Over the past several years, organizations have increasingly adopted artificial intelligence (AI) to augment their capabilities, improve efficiency, and drive innovation. In particular, investments in generative and predictive AI technologies have surged, reflecting a widespread belief that AI can act as a force multiplier, enabling individuals and teams to achieve greater outcomes without a proportional increase in effort or resources.

Despite this promise, many organizations are failing to realize the expected returns from their AI initiatives. While the technical capabilities of AI systems have advanced rapidly, the ability of organizations to integrate these tools effectively into everyday business operations has not kept pace. This gap is often the result of persistent organizational constraints such as rigid budgeting structures, low-quality data, slow decision-making processes, and workforce skill gaps. These limitations can absorb or even negate the potential value AI might otherwise deliver.

This paper explores how AI's impact is shaped by organizational readiness and internal constraints. It presents findings from a Delphi study involving experts from across industries, examining both the barriers that limit AI success and the business capabilities that can unlock its full potential. The goal is to offer practical guidance for business and technology leaders seeking to maximize the strategic benefits of AI, not through technical upgrades alone, but by fostering adaptive, human-centric organizational systems.

2 Methodology

2.1 Research Design

This study employed the Delphi method, a structured and iterative process used to gather insights and achieve consensus among a panel of experts. The method is particularly well-suited for exploring emerging topics where direct evidence may be limited, but informed expert opinion can offer valuable direction. The Delphi approach also enabled the synthesis of diverse perspectives through multiple rounds of feedback, thereby enhancing the reliability and validity of the findings.

2.2 Expert Panel Composition

The expert panel consisted of 18 individuals with significant experience in either artificial intelligence (AI) implementation or business agility transformation. Panelists represented a broad cross-section of industries, including technology, telecommunications, aerospace, healthcare, and consulting. Participants were identified through peer recommendations, professional networks, and affiliations with known industry bodies. The panel also included senior leaders and domain experts such as chief technology officers, AI product engineers, and transformation consultants.

To encourage open and candid feedback, participation was voluntary, and anonymity was preserved in published results where requested.

2.3 Data Collection and Analysis

The study was conducted over four iterative rounds:

Round 1 involved open-ended questions to elicit initial perspectives on AI adoption, expected outcomes, organizational constraints, and relevant business capabilities.

Round 2 presented a thematic summary of responses from Round 1. Panelists were asked to reflect on the collective input, prioritize key issues, and clarify areas of disagreement or uncertainty.

Round 3 refined the findings, focusing on achieving consensus regarding the most critical constraints limiting AI's potential and the capabilities most effective in overcoming them.

Round 4 consisted of facilitated group calls to validate open questions and ensure alignment across responses.

Quantitative and qualitative data were collected in each round. Thematic analysis was applied to qualitative responses to identify common patterns and concepts. Quantitative items, such as constraint severity ratings and capability impact scores, were summarized using descriptive statistics. Discrepancies in responses were retained for interpretation and discussion, providing a balanced view of consensus and divergence.

2.4 Ethical Considerations

All participants provided informed consent prior to participation. Data was anonymized and stored securely, accessible only to the research team. No identifying details about individuals or organizations were shared in the final analysis without explicit permission.

3 Key Findings

3.1 The Promise of AI as a Force Multiplier

The expert panel identified that AI, when effectively integrated, has the potential to serve as a force multiplier, amplifying the effectiveness of individuals, teams, and organizations without requiring equivalent increases in resources. Across the study, AI was seen to enhance value in three primary business areas:

- **Product and Service Delivery**
  AI accelerates product development cycles, improves product quality, and enables greater innovation. Expert estimates indicated potential performance gains ranging from 1.4 to 2.7 times in this domain.
- **Business Operations**
  AI improves operational efficiency by streamlining workflows, enhancing decision-making, and reducing overhead. The estimated impact ranged from 1.2 to 2.5 times.
- **Customer Engagement**
  AI-driven personalization and availability improvements were projected to yield gains between 1.4 and 2.8 times, particularly in customer satisfaction and responsiveness.

However, the realized multiplier effect varied dramatically from modest improvements of 1.2x to transformative gains of over 3x, depending on an organization's internal capability to adopt, integrate, and scale AI effectively.

3.2 Organizational Constraints

Despite high levels of investment and interest, many organizations fail to realize the full potential of their AI initiatives. The expert panel identified six recurring constraints that consistently limited the success of AI efforts:

1. **Rigid Budgeting Cycles**
   Annual, plan-based budgets hinder the ability to fund emergent opportunities uncovered through AI tools.
2. **Poor Data Quality**
   Legacy systems, fragmented data practices, and inadequate governance result in unreliable or biased AI outputs.
3. **Slow or Committee-Based Decision-Making**
   Strategic paralysis often occurs when leaders either overestimate or underestimate the capabilities of AI, leading to delays in implementation.
4. **Disproportionate Bureaucracy**
   Overly complex compliance structures slow innovation, while the lack of clear governance introduces risk and uncertainty.
5. **Low Trust in AI Outputs**
   Hallucinations, inconsistencies, and over-reliance on AI without human oversight erode trust and hinder adoption.

6. **Gaps in Workforce Talent**
Most employees lack the emerging skills required to effectively collaborate with AI systems. This includes prompt engineering, critical evaluation of AI outputs, and integration into existing workflows.

These constraints not only absorb potential benefits but also lead to disillusionment and, in some cases, the abandonment of AI initiatives before value is realized.

3.3 Capability Gaps and the Realization Gap

Even in organizations with advanced AI technologies, the benefits are limited when foundational business capabilities are lacking. The gap between AI's theoretical potential and its realized impact is often due to the mismatch between the system's speed and organizational readiness. For example, while predictive AI might generate insights instantly, organizational decision-making cycles may still take weeks.

The panel emphasized that AI can only accelerate what the organization is already capable of executing. Without the capacity to respond dynamically—through flexible funding, fast decision-making, and agile workflows—the benefits of AI are absorbed by systemic friction. Furthermore, AI often amplifies existing inefficiencies or bottlenecks, worsening outcomes unless organizations actively resolve their most limiting constraints.

4 Enabling Capabilities

While technical AI proficiency is essential, the expert panel emphasized that business outcomes are ultimately determined by an organization's ability to integrate AI into its structures, workflows, and culture. AI does not operate in a vacuum; it amplifies existing systems and behaviors. Therefore, unlocking AI's potential requires targeted development of human-centered business capabilities.

Drawing from the Domains of Business Agility model, the panel identified seven capabilities as the most effective for addressing the common organizational constraints limiting AI's impact. These capabilities enable organizations to adapt, align, and act at the speed of AI.

These seven capabilities offer a practical roadmap for organizations seeking to transform AI from a theoretical advantage into measurable outcomes. When developed intentionally, they address the root causes of underperformance and unlock the full value of AI as a force multiplier.

4.1 Cultivating a Learning Organization

Organizations that embrace continuous learning are better positioned to absorb and adapt to AI-driven change. A strong learning culture fosters innovation, enhances employee engagement, and mitigates resistance to new technologies. Teams are encouraged to experiment, learn from failures, and iterate quickly; critical behaviors for realizing AI's transformative potential.

Without these cultural foundations, organizations risk falling behind, misinterpreting AI's potential, or investing in tools they are not equipped to use effectively.

4.2 Unleashing Workflow Creatively

Rigid, siloed workflows are one of the biggest barriers to AI integration. Every handoff, delay, or manual step introduces friction that AI cannot solve. Organizations that prioritize end-to-end workflow design, eliminate unnecessary approvals, connect systems, and integrate AI into core processes can dramatically increase both speed and impact.

Creative workflow design shifts the focus from maximizing local efficiency to achieving system-wide effectiveness, which is essential for scaling AI outcomes.

4.3 Sense and Respond Proactively

AI excels at detecting patterns across data sources, but its value is limited unless organizations can act on those signals. The ability to sense emerging trends and respond in real time is a key differentiator in AI maturity. Agile organizations build feedback loops that inform decisions early, allowing them to test, validate, and pivot with confidence.

Proactive sensing enables leaders to avoid the "wait and see" trap and instead seize opportunities before competitors do.

4.4 Prioritize. Prioritize. Prioritize.

The expansive possibilities offered by AI can overwhelm teams without a clear strategic focus. Organizations must prioritize initiatives that align with business goals and customer needs; otherwise, resources are spread too thin or wasted on low-value efforts.

Effective prioritization enables faster decisions, clearer team alignment, and more impactful use of AI. Leadership plays a crucial role in continually reevaluating and communicating what matters most.

4.5 Fund Work Dynamically

Traditional budget models are too slow and rigid to support AI-driven opportunities, which often emerge unpredictably. Dynamic funding approaches, such as rolling budgets, platform-based investments, or outcome-based allocation, enable organizations to reallocate resources quickly and capitalize on AI insights.

Without financial agility, even the best AI-generated ideas may stall due to a lack of timely support.

4.6 Realize People's Potential

AI is most effective when paired with skilled, empowered individuals. Upskilling employees to work as "composers" of AI—guiding inputs, interpreting outputs, and ensuring alignment with business context—is essential. At the same time, organizations must determine whether to train existing staff or hire new talent, striking a balance between continuity and fresh expertise.

People who are confident in their ability to collaborate with AI can elevate both their own performance and organizational outcomes.

4.7 Balancing Governance and Risk

AI introduces new ethical, legal, and operational risks that require careful oversight. But heavy-handed governance can paralyze innovation. The most effective organizations implement lightweight, adaptive frameworks that ensure AI outputs are accurate, compliant, and ethical, without creating unnecessary barriers to experimentation.

By striking the right balance, leaders can build stakeholder trust while enabling fast, responsible innovation.

5 Discussion

This study affirms that the effectiveness of artificial intelligence in organizations is not limited by the technology itself, but by the systems into which it is introduced. While AI can generate extraordinary speed, scale, and insight, its value is ultimately governed by an organization's ability to absorb and act on that output.

One of the clearest distinctions emerging from this research is between augmentation and automation. The majority of successful AI use cases were not those that attempted to replace humans, but those that amplified human capacity. When AI is used to enhance human judgment, creativity, or speed, it delivers far greater return on investment than when applied to tasks better suited to traditional automation technologies. This principle reframes AI as a collaborative partner, not a standalone replacement.

This shift requires a redefinition of roles. Instead of serving solely as content creators or decision-makers, individuals must learn to operate as composers, curating inputs, managing prompts, and critically evaluating outputs. In this new mode of work, success depends less on technical fluency and more on adaptability, judgment, and orchestration. As one panelist noted, "AI is like an unlimited number of junior engineers working with you." It is up to the human leader to direct that capacity wisely.

These insights also highlight the risks associated with superficial AI adoption. When organizations pursue AI without addressing the underlying constraints, such as slow decision-making, rigid funding, or disconnected workflows, they risk amplifying dysfunction rather than solving it. AI does not eliminate friction in a system; it accelerates whatever system it's embedded in, for better or worse.

The findings reinforce the strategic importance of capability development, particularly in areas that enable responsiveness, alignment, and learning. Without these, organizations will remain stuck in a cycle of stalled pilots, unmet expectations, and misallocated investments.

Ultimately, the question is not whether AI can deliver value, but whether organizations are prepared to receive it.

6 Conclusion

Artificial intelligence holds immense promise as a force multiplier in business, capable of improving speed, quality, and innovation across nearly every domain. Yet, as this study shows, most organizations are not yet positioned to fully capture that value. The gap between AI's potential and its realized impact is not primarily technical; it is organizational.

Through a Delphi-based investigation involving cross-industry experts, this paper identifies the primary constraints undermining AI initiatives: rigid funding models, fragmented workflows, poor data quality, and unprepared workforces. It also highlights seven human-centered capabilities that enable organizations to overcome these constraints, including the ability to prioritize effectively, respond dynamically, and cultivate continuous learning.

The path forward requires a mindset shift from implementing AI as a tool to orchestrating it as a collaborative partner. Leaders must focus less on deployment timelines and more on developing the business capabilities that allow AI to thrive. They must rethink what constitutes good work, how performance is evaluated, and how teams learn and adapt.

In doing so, AI becomes more than a technology layer. It becomes an accelerant of human potential, enabling organizations not only to work faster but to work better.

Acknowledgments. Considerable thanks and appreciation go to Laura Powers, CEO, Business Agility Institute and Peter Lam, Australia, Principal – Transformation, Claritas Consulting for the time and effort they provided in the review and support in the authoring of this report. Their feedback was invaluable to the composition and finding of this report.

Additionally, we gratefully acknowledge the time, expertise, and insight shared by the expert panel who contributed to this study. Their diverse perspectives from fields including artificial intelligence, organizational transformation, aerospace, telecommunications, healthcare, and technology made this work possible. The participants included:

- Pete Behrens, USA, Founder and CEO, Agile Leadership Journey.
- Dr. Ferenc Birloni, Australia, Partner, PHI Institute for Augmented Intelligence.
- Debbie Brey, USA, Technical Fellow, Aerospace Company.
- Bill Dominguez, USA, Founder and CEO, Ecocentric Strategies.
- Dr. Marwane El Kharbili, Germany, AI Product Engineer, WOMAT.
- Giles Lindsay, UK, Chief Information and Technology Officer (CITO), Lif3away.
- Peter Merel, Australia, Founder, XSCALE Alliance.
- Stuart Munton, UK, CIO | Chief for Group Operations & Technology, AND Digital.
- Andrew Park, USA, Founder, Edensoft Labs.
- Paula Riano, New Zealand, Gen AI Change Program Lead, Spark.
- Tony Ta, Australia, Co-Founder, olla.ai.
- John Tanner, USA, Chief Strategist, C4G Enterprises.
- Dr. Jess Tayel, Australia, Founder, Transformation Leadership Institute.

Three expert panel members requested to remain anonymous in the final report.

Disclosure of Interests. The authors have no competing interests to declare that are relevant to the content of this article.

Reference. No external sources were cited in this study. All findings are based on original research conducted by the authors and the Business Agility Institute expert panel

Open Access This chapter is licensed under the terms of the Creative Commons Attribution 4.0 International License (http://creativecommons.org/licenses/by/4.0/), which permits use, sharing, adaptation, distribution and reproduction in any medium or format, as long as you give appropriate credit to the original author(s) and the source, provide a link to the Creative Commons license and indicate if changes were made.

The images or other third party material in this chapter are included in the chapter's Creative Commons license, unless indicated otherwise in a credit line to the material. If material is not included in the chapter's Creative Commons license and your intended use is not permitted by statutory regulation or exceeds the permitted use, you will need to obtain permission directly from the copyright holder.

Why Adapt RAG for Agile? Challenges, Frameworks, and the Role of Evaluator Agent

Ayman Asad Khan[✉], Md Toufique Hasan, Mika Saari,
Kai-Kristian Kemell, and Jussi Rasku

Tampere University, Tampere, Finland
{ayman.khan,mdtoufique.hasan,mika.saari,
kai-kristian.kemell,jussi.rasku}@tuni.f

Abstract. This paper proposes the adaptation of Retrieval Augmented Generation (RAG) based systems into Agile Software Development workflows, addressing the need for specialized evaluation methods that align with Agile's iterative, feedback driven nature. Through a systematic mapping study of 20 papers, we identify existing evaluation frameworks for RAG systems and explore how they can be applied within Agile settings. The research highlights the role of Evaluator-Agents in aligning the responsiveness of RAG systems, with a focus on Multi-agent AI systems that are more efficient at handling complex, distributed tasks than Single-agent systems. The findings contribute to identify the potential of RAG and its evaluation in facilitating real time feedback and continuous improvement for Agile development.

Keywords: AI · Agile · Retrieval-Augmented Generation (RAG) · Large Language Models (LLMs) · Multi-agent · Evaluation · Mapping-Study

1 Introduction

Generative Artificial Intelligence (Gen-AI) tools such as ChatGPT, GitHub Copilot, and others have showcased impressive capabilities in tasks ranging from code generation to project management. This growth has facilitated research into novel AI applications, including its integration into Multi-agent Systems and Evaluator-Agent implementations [18]. However, most Gen-AI tools or systems have a lot of knowledge which is static and monolithic, it can't easily learn new things or explain where the information is from to meet the needs of dynamic environments.

Agile methodologies, on the other side, prioritize iterative, feedback driven development and adaptability, which are central to the continuous delivery of software. The emphasis on rapid cycles of development, testing, and feedback makes Agile environments dynamic and fast paced, requiring real time responsiveness from AI systems. Retrieval Augmented Generation (RAG) can address this fundamental limitations in current Gen-AI and Agile integration. RAG combines retrieval mechanism in real time from external data sources as additional knowledge to the Large Language Models (LLMs) grounding the accuracy and relevance of AI generated outputs.

This paper thus aims to explore the adaptation and potential of RAG based LLM systems into Agile workflows. The focus of this study is twofold. **RQ1** aims to identify the existing evaluation frameworks for RAG systems, examining the methodologies and metrics used to assess their effectiveness. **RQ2** explores how these frameworks can be integrated into Agile Software Development workflows, with particular attention to the challenges posed by Agile's emphasis on flexibility, continuous feedback, and iterative improvement.

RQ1: What existing evaluation frameworks for Retrieval Augmented Generation (RAG) systems can be identified?

RQ2: How can existing RAG evaluation frameworks be adapted to Agile Software Development workflows?

This study contributes to the growing body of research on Gen-AI and Agile by systematically mapping the existing evaluation frameworks for RAG systems and identifying how these frameworks can be adapted for use within Agile Development. It highlights how Multi-agent Systems, particularly Evaluator-Agents, can support real-time, context-sensitive feedback and continuous improvement, ensuring RAG systems align with Agile's iterative and collaborative nature.

2 Related Work

LLMs generate human-like content [4] across modalities by learning from large datasets via transformer architectures [25]. Despite their capabilities, LLMs are limited by their inability to access real-time or domain-specific information, reducing their adaptability in dynamic environments. RAG introduced by Lewis et al. [15] overcomes this by fusing retrieval and generation: external data is fetched and injected into the LLM, yielding more accurate, context-aware outputs in tasks such as Q&A and dialogue (see Fig. 1).

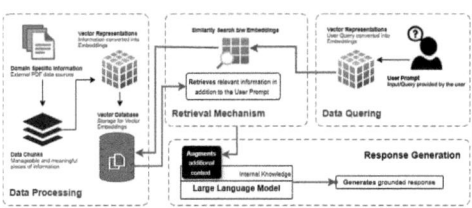

Fig. 1. Retrieval-Augmented Generation (RAG) Mechanism

Despite clear potential, the use of Gen-AI, RAG, and Multi-agent Systems in Agile Software Development (ASD) remains underexplored. Agile's core values:

flexibility, iteration, and continuous feedback [3], align well with AI, suggesting benefits like automated code generation, real-time decision support, and faster feedback loops. Multi-agent ecosystems such as CogniSim (Chudziak et al. [8]) show how autonomous developer, QA, and methodology agents can collaborate, share external knowledge, and provide sprint-level feedback. Zhang et al. [26] further highlight multi-agent use of historical data for automated user-story generation and testing.

Integrating RAG and multi-agent systems into Agile workflows can close feedback loops, enhance collaboration, and boost product quality through continuous, context-aware adaptation

3 Methodology

This study employs a systematic mapping study as the research method. It classifies and structures a specific field of interest, analyzing publication frequencies to determine research coverage. Following guidelines by Petersen et al. [20], to create the systematic map and identify key landmarks, the study selection process was carried out in several stages for a focused analysis of the relevant research. It helped provide valuable insights even when empirical evidence on the integration of RAG in Agile methodologies was limited. We structured the process in five stages (Fig. 2):

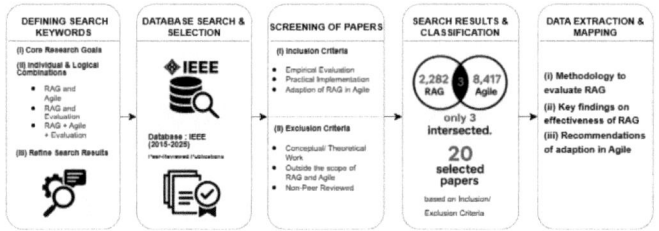

Fig. 2. Systematic Mapping Study

Defining Search Keywords: We began by identifying keywords related to the research goals of this paper. Terms were drawn from the domains of RAG, Agile Software Development, and evaluation methodologies as illustrated in Table 1. Keywords were used both individually and in combination (e.g., *RAG* and *Agile*, *RAG* and *Evaluation*, *RAG + Agile + Evaluation*).

Database Search and Selection: IEEE Xplore (2015–2025) was selected for its coverage of peer-reviewed literature in AI and software engineering, including topics relevant to LLMs, RAG, and Agile methodologies. The database was selected and narrowed down based on the inclusion criteria.

Screening of Papers for Inclusion and Exclusion: We screened the retrieved papers based on predefined inclusion and exclusion criteria:

- **Inclusion Criteria:** Studies that explore evaluation frameworks for RAG systems, Agile development methods, or AI integration in Agile were included. Additionally, papers that propose adaptations of evaluation frameworks for RAG in Agile workflows were considered highly relevant.
- **Exclusion Criteria:** Papers that focused solely on theoretical or conceptual work without empirical evaluation or practical application in Agile environments, or papers outside the scope of RAG and Gen-AI, were excluded.

Search Results and Classification Scheme: From an initial pool of thousands as shown in Table 1, we shortlisted **20 articles** based on relevance to our RQs. Studies were classified according to the type of evaluation (e.g., performance, usability, feedback loops, etc.). We categorized the studies by their contribution to the field, including empirical studies, solution proposals, or theoretical frameworks.

Table 1. Search Keywords and Results (from 2015–2025)

Concept	Keywords	Results
RAG	Retrieval Augmented Generation **OR** RAG **OR** Information retrieval in AI systems.	2,282
Agile Software Development	Agile software development **OR** Agile workflows **OR** Agile testing and feedback.	8,417
Evaluation Frameworks	Large Language Model evaluation **OR** Evaluation frameworks for RAG models **OR** Evaluation agents for LLMs **OR** AI agents for model evaluation.	5,098
	("Retrieval Augmented Generation" **OR** RAG) **AND** Agile.	3
	("Retrieval Augmented Generation" **OR** RAG) **AND** Evaluation.	159
	("Retrieval Augmented Generation" **OR** RAG) **AND** Agile **AND** Evaluation.	1

Data Extraction and Mapping Process: For each selected paper, we recorded the evaluation methodology, application domain, and alignment with Agile feedback principles.

4 Results

4.1 RQ1: Existing Evaluation Frameworks for RAG Systems

We identified several evaluation frameworks for RAG systems, each designed to assess performance, usability, quality, and accuracy (see Table 2). These range from general-purpose benchmarks to domain-specific evaluations for tasks such as question answering and specialized knowledge retrieval. They offer key insights into how RAG outputs can meet real-world standards of relevance and coherence.

Hamzic et al. [12] evaluate RAG-based LLMs using NLG metrics like BLEU and ROUGE, alongside human assessments, focusing on response accuracy and coherence. This provides a standardized approach for general-purpose RAG evaluation. Kukreja et al. [14] assess vector embedding performance within RAG systems, emphasizing semantic search effectiveness in retrieving and generating relevant content. Sun et al. [23] introduce a multimodal evaluation framework for RAG systems handling text, images, and video. They focus on accuracy, noise robustness, and response quality–critical for complex, real-world, mixed-data environments.

Kenneweg et al. [13] present RAGVAL, a data-centric framework that automates dataset creation for evaluating RAG models, prioritizing relevance, diversity, and knowledge integration–an often overlooked but crucial aspect of RAG performance. Cenić et al. [7] explore a Serbian-language hybrid search RAG system, combining keyword and semantic search to enhance contextual accuracy in non-English settings. Li et al. [16] apply RAG to medical reasoning using meta-questions to guide domain-specific retrieval and generation, improving accuracy in specialized fields like dermatology.

Saha et al. [22] propose Inverted Question Matching (IQM) to evaluate QA performance, focusing on hallucination mitigation and retrieval precision. Abrahamyan et al. [1] introduce the StackRAG Agent, which enhances developer tools using Stack Overflow data, measuring the accuracy and relevance of automated responses for software maintenance. Sundar et al. [24] emphasize context modeling in education-focused RAG evaluation, while Hammane et al. [11] propose a self-evaluating model for medical reasoning, where the system assesses its own outputs to improve decision-making.

Collectively, these frameworks demonstrate a strong foundation for evaluating RAG systems across diverse applications. Their methodologies, metrics, and adaptability offer valuable starting points for integrating real-time evaluation into Agile Software Development workflows, discussed next in **RQ2**.

4.2 RQ2: Adaptation of RAG Evaluation Frameworks to Agile

Adapting RAG evaluation frameworks to Agile hinges on continuous, sprint-level feedback supplied by autonomous Evaluator-Agents. Paliwal et al. [19] explore how Gen-AI can accelerate time-to-market in product development, emphasizing the role of AI in collaborative environments and rapid prototyping. Conventional, linear RAG assessments must evolve into agent-driven cycles that check outputs

Table 2. Categorization of RAG Evaluation Frameworks

Framework	Purpose	Evaluation Criteria	Application Domain
Hamzic et al. [12]	Quality Evaluation	Accuracy, Coherence, Reliability	General purpose NLG tasks
Kukreja et al. [14]	Performance Evaluation	Speed, Accuracy, Scalability	Semantic search, Querying, NLP tasks
Sun et al. [23]	Multimodal Evaluation	Accuracy, Noise Robustness, Quality of Response	Multimodal applications (Text, Image, Video)
Kenneweg et al. [13]	Automated Dataset Creation and Evaluation	Dataset Quality, Accuracy, Contextual Relevance	Data centric applications, Knowledge management
Cenić et al. [7]	Quality Evaluation	Accuracy, Contextual Understanding	Historical and Cultural Knowledge Systems (Serbian)
Li et al. [16]	Domain Specific Evaluation	Domain Specific Accuracy, Contextual Precision	Medical applications (Dermatology)
Saha et al. [22]	Performance Evaluation in QA	Accuracy, Hallucination Mitigation, Information Dilution	Question Answering Systems (QA), LLMs
Abrahamyan et al. [1]	Performance Evaluation in Developer Tools	Accuracy, Relevance, Reliability	Software Maintenance, Developer Tools (e.g., Stack Overflow)
Sundar et al. [24]	Education Evaluation	Accuracy, Contextual Modeling, Reliability	Education, Assessment Systems
Hammane et al. [11]	Medical Reasoning Evaluation	Decision Making, Accuracy, Real time Integration	Medical Reasoning, Healthcare

against sprint goals after each iteration. Below, we discuss how each framework can be adapted for Agile workflows, with a focus on the role of Evaluator-agents in facilitating feedback-driven improvement.

In Rauf and AlGhafees [21], a gap analysis identifies where current Agile practices lack real time feedback and continuous integration. Evaluator-agents can fill this gap by monitoring backlog, task progress, and integration. In cloud-security (Cao and Jun [5]) or benchmarked LLM agents (Dong et al. [21]), agents track performance, perform vulnerability detection and adapt models on-the-fly.

In Ågren et al. [27], the authors propose extending Agile practices beyond software teams into cross-functional settings, such as automotive systems, which include both hardware and software engineering. This approach requires continuous feedback across multiple teams. Moreover, Aoki et al. [2] highlight the application of LLM-based narrative generation using agent-based simulation for evaluating narrative coherence and decision-making accuracy. Simulation-based agents maintain collaboration efficiency across disciplines.

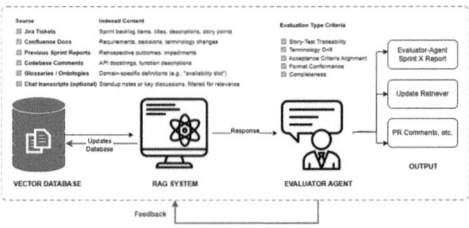

Fig. 3. Use Case of Evaluator-Agent with RAG in Agile.

Multi-agent RAG chatbots for net-zero energy (Gamage et al. [10]), Agile project management automation (Dhruva et al. [9]), and educational/team evaluation (Miranda et al. [17]) all gain from agents that flag context drift and accuracy issues. In Cassieri et al. [6], Gen-AI is applied to Test-Driven Development (TDD), where RAG systems generate test cases to ensure software quality.

Agile emphasizes not just speed but continuous course correction. To align RAG systems with Agile workflows, we propose integrating **Evaluator-Agents** that assess both the textual accuracy of outputs and their alignment with sprint goals. These agents require access to project artifacts such as backlogs, issue trackers, and prompt-response logs, and can optionally leverage domain ontologies to assess contextual relevance. *For example,* as shown in Fig. 3 an Evaluator-Agent is integrated into the CI/CD pipeline and is triggered automatically to perform different categories of evaluations.

5 Discussion

Agile research is abundant (over 8,417 studies), yet work at the application of RAG systems within Agile environments remains under explored. Only a handful of studies (3) have focused on the intersection of these two fields. Although over 5,000 publications discuss RAG evaluation, few address Agile's iterative demands. This gap signals the need for frameworks that blend continuous feedback with iterative evaluation.

One of the key findings of this study is that current RAG evaluation frameworks are not fully aligned with Agile environments. They focus primarily on static, performance based testing and do not consider the continuous feedback loops and real time evaluations that Agile demands. Frameworks such as Hamzic et al. [12] and Kukreja et al. [14] provide useful insights into NLG quality and semantic search performance, but they lack the ability to facilitate real time evaluation and continuous improvement. This indicates that while these frameworks serve as important baselines, they require adaptation to align with Agile's feedback driven nature. A key adaptation is the inclusion of the role of Evaluator-agents, autonomous agents that can track RAG performance, dynamic evaluation and provide real time feedback, enabling the iterative refinement required in Agile workflows. In collaborative settings, Multi-agent Systems can coordinate these evaluations, ensuring consistent performance tracking and feedback across the Agile workflow.

The challenges of adapting RAG evaluation frameworks to Agile workflows include the inherent complexity of RAG systems and the difficulty in measuring their real-time performance. RAG systems require constant adaptation to new data inputs, making it difficult to assess their performance using traditional, static evaluation methods. This challenge is compounded in Agile environments, where feedback needs to be provided rapidly and on an ongoing basis, not at the end of a lengthy evaluation process.

This study's scope (single database, empirical focus) limits coverage; future work should broaden sources (e.g., ACM, Springer) and investigate how evaluation agents improve RAG adaptability within Agile contexts.

Future Research Question: What role do evaluation agents play in improving the adaptability of RAG systems in Agile environments

6 Concluding Remarks

In conclusion, this systematic mapping study of 20 articles identified existing RAG evaluation frameworks and explored their adaptation to Agile Software Development workflows. The findings highlight the need for real time feedback and continuous evaluation in Agile environments, which current frameworks lack. We propose the integration of Evaluator-agents to ensure iterative refinement and dynamic adaptation of RAG systems in Agile cycles. This work contributes to the understanding of how RAG systems can be effectively evaluated within Agile frameworks, offering practical insights for future research and application. Future work should focus on empirical testing of the adapted frameworks in real world Agile environments and the development of new frameworks tailored specifically to the unique challenges of integrating RAG systems with Agile principles.

References

1. Abrahamyan, D., Fard, F.H.: StackRAG agent: improving developer answers with retrieval-augmented generation. In: 2024 IEEE International Conference on Software Maintenance and Evolution (ICSME), pp. 893–897 (2024)
2. Aoki, N., Mori, N., OKada, M.: Analysis of LLM-based narrative generation using the agent-based simulation. In: 2023 15th International Congress on Advanced Applied Informatics Winter (IIAI-AAI-Winter), pp. 284–289 (2023)
3. Beck, K.L., et al.: Manifesto for agile software development (2013)
4. Brown, T.B., et al.: Language models are few-shot learners (2020)
5. Cao, D., Jun, W.: LLM-CloudSec: large language model empowered automatic and deep vulnerability analysis for intelligent clouds. In: IEEE INFOCOM 2024 - IEEE Conference on Computer Communications Workshops (INFOCOM WKSHPS), pp. 1–6 (2024)

6. Cassieri, P., Romano, S., Scanniello, G.: Generative artificial intelligence for test-driven development: GAI4- TDD. In: 2024 IEEE International Conference on Software Analysis, Evolution and Reengineering (SANER), pp. 902–906 (2024)
7. Cenić, A., Jovanović, M., Stojković, S.: The Serbian retrieval augmented generation system based on hybrid search. In: 2024 International Conference Automatics and Informatics (ICAI), pp. 420–424 (2024)
8. Chudziak, J.A., Cinkusz, K.: Towards LLM-augmented multiagent systems for agile software engineering. In: 2024 39th IEEE/ACM International Conference on Automated Software Engineering (ASE), pp. 2476–2477 (2024)
9. Dhruva, G., Shettigar, I., Parthasarthy, S., Sapna, V.M.: Agile project management using large language models. In: 2024 5th International Conference on Innovative Trends in Information Technology (ICITIIT), pp. 1–6 (2024)
10. Gamage, G., et al.: Multi-agent rag chatbot architecture for decision support in net-zero emission energy systems. In: 2024 IEEE International Conference on Industrial Technology (ICIT), pp. 1–6 (2024)
11. Hammane, Z., Ben-Bouazza, F.E., Fennan, A.: SelfRewardRAG: enhancing medical reasoning with retrieval-augmented generation and self-evaluation in large language models. In: 2024 International Conference on Intelligent Systems and Computer Vision (ISCV), pp. 1–8 (2024)
12. Hamzic, D., Wurzenberger, M., Skopik, F., Landauer, M., Rauber, A.: Evaluation and comparison of open-source LLMs using natural language generation quality metrics. In: 2024 IEEE International Conference on Big Data (BigData), pp. 5342–5351 (2024)
13. Kenneweg, T., Kenneweg, P., Hammer, B.: RAGVAL: automatic dataset creation and evaluation for rag systems. In: 2024 2nd International Conference on Foundation and Large Language Models (FLLM), pp. 470–475 (2024)
14. Kukreja, S., Kumar, T., Bharate, V., Purohit, A., Dasgupta, A., Guha, D.: Performance evaluation of vector embeddings with retrieval-augmented generation. In: 2024 9th International Conference on Computer and Communication Systems (ICCCS), pp. 333–340 (2024)
15. Lewis, P., et al.: Retrieval-augmented generation for knowledge-intensive NLP tasks. In: Proceedings of the 34th International Conference on Neural Information Processing Systems, NIPS 2020. Curran Associates Inc., Red Hook (2020)
16. Li, C., et al.: Development of a meta-question enhanced retrieval-augmented generation model and its application in dermatology. In: 2024 17th International Conference on Advanced Computer Theory and Engineering (ICACTE), pp. 281–285 (2024)
17. Miranda, D., Palma, D., Fernández, A., Noel, R., Cechinel, C., Munoz, R.: Enhancing agile project management education with AI: CHATGPT-4's role in evaluating student contributions. In: 2024 43rd International Conference of the Chilean Computer Science Society (SCCC), pp. 1–4 (2024)
18. Nguyen-Duc, A., et al.: Generative artificial intelligence for software engineering – a research agenda (2023)
19. Paliwal, G., Donvir, A., Gujar, P., Panyam, S.: Accelerating time-to-market: the role of generative AI in product development. In: 2024 IEEE Colombian Conference on Communications and Computing (COLCOM), pp. 1–9 (2024)
20. Petersen, K., Feldt, R., Mujtaba, S., Mattsson, M.: Systematic mapping studies in software engineering. In: International Conference on Evaluation & Assessment in Software Engineering (2008)

21. Rauf, A., AlGhafees, M.: Gap analysis between state of practice and state of art practices in agile software development. In: 2015 Agile Conference, pp. 102–106 (2015)
22. Saha, B., Saha, U., Zubair Malik, M.: QuIM-RAG: advancing retrieval-augmented generation with inverted question matching for enhanced QA performance. IEEE Access **12**, 185401–185410 (2024)
23. Sun, T., Somalwar, A., Chan, H.: Multimodal retrieval augmented generation evaluation benchmark. In: 2024 IEEE 99th Vehicular Technology Conference (VTC2024-Spring), pp. 1–5 (2024)
24. Sundar, K., Manohar, E., Vijay, K., Prakash, S.: Revolutionizing assessment: AI-powered evaluation with rag and LLM technologies. In: 2024 2nd International Conference on Self Sustainable Artificial Intelligence Systems (ICSSAS), pp. 43–48 (2024)
25. Vaswani, A., et al.: Attention is all you need (2023)
26. Zhang, Z., Rayhan, M., Herda, T., Goisauf, M., Abrahamsson, P.: LLM-based agents for automating the enhancement of user story quality: an early report. In: Šmite, D., Guerra, E., Wang, X., Marchesi, M., Gregory, P. (eds.) Agile Processes in Software Engineering and Extreme Programming, pp. 117–126. Springer, Cham (2024)
27. Ågren, S.M., Heldal, R., Knauss, E., Pelliccione, P.: Agile beyond teams and feedback beyond software in automotive systems. IEEE Trans. Eng. Manage. **69**(6), 3459–3475 (2022)

Open Access This chapter is licensed under the terms of the Creative Commons Attribution 4.0 International License (http://creativecommons.org/licenses/by/4.0/), which permits use, sharing, adaptation, distribution and reproduction in any medium or format, as long as you give appropriate credit to the original author(s) and the source, provide a link to the Creative Commons license and indicate if changes were made.

The images or other third party material in this chapter are included in the chapter's Creative Commons license, unless indicated otherwise in a credit line to the material. If material is not included in the chapter's Creative Commons license and your intended use is not permitted by statutory regulation or exceeds the permitted use, you will need to obtain permission directly from the copyright holder.

AI and Teamwork in Agile Software Development: A Systematic Mapping Study

Ya Ting Crystal Kwok(✉) and Mahum Adil

Free University of Bozen-Bolzano, Bolzano, Italy
`kwokyatingcrystal@gmail.com, mahum.adil@student.unibz.it`

Abstract. *Background.* Agile software development relies on effective teamwork to achieve successful project outcomes. While the integration of Artificial Intelligence (AI) into Agile practices has gained attention, its specific role in supporting teamwork remains relatively underexplored. *Aim.* This study provides a systematic overview of current research on AI in Agile teamwork, focusing on the 3Cs of teamwork: communication, collaboration, and coordination. *Method.* We conducted a Systematic Mapping Study (SMS) analyzing research studies published from January 2001 to January 2025. *Result.* Among the limited body of research focusing on teamwork, the studies are well distributed across the 3C aspects. Natural language processing (NLP) is the most widely studied AI technology, while large language models (LLM) remain underexplored. Furthermore, relatively few studies investigate higher-autonomy AI roles, such as agents and assistants. *Conclusion.* This study highlights key research gaps and suggests future opportunities to leverage advanced AI technologies to enhance teamwork in Agile software development.

Keywords: Agile Software Development · Artificial Intelligence · Teamwork · Communication · Collaboration · Coordination

1 Introduction

Agile software development has transformed how software is built, enabling teams to adapt to change, enhance collaboration, and deliver software products iteratively [1]. Across industries, organizations have adopted Agile frameworks such as Scrum, Kanban, and Extreme Programming (XP) to improve flexibility, responsiveness, and team efficiency [2]. One of the core values of Agile, as outlined in the Agile Manifesto [3], is that individuals and interactions are valued over processes and tools. This, therefore, establishes teamwork – how teams collaborate, communicate, and coordinate – as a crucial part of Agile practices [4].

Artificial Intelligence (AI) has advanced significantly, revolutionizing various domains, including Agile software development [5]. AI applications extend beyond automation to support tasks such as bug detection, predictive analytics, and AI-powered assistants or chatbots that streamline workflows [6]. AI-driven techniques like machine learning (ML) and natural language processing (NLP) are increasingly integrated into Agile software development to enhance productivity and efficiency [7].

2 Related Work

In recent years, research on AI in Agile software development has increased, with most studies focusing on improving workflows, processes and tools [6–8]. However, the exploration into AI in teamwork, one of the core aspect of Agile software development, remains unclear, as far as the authors are aware of.

On the other hand, research on teamwork in Agile software development has been well-established. Strode et al. [9] proposed the Agile Teamwork Effectiveness Model (ATEM) to identify key factors contributing to teamwork effectiveness while Hoda et al. [1] examined the evolution of Agile software development, tracing its historical development, adoption, and transformation across industries. While these studies provide valuable insights into teamwork, they do not investigate the use of AI in teamwork in Agile software development.

This research gap highlights the need to examine AI's role in teamwork in Agile software development, referred to as Agile teamwork in this study. Building on existing systematic mapping studies, this study provides an overview of AI's role in Agile teamwork, specifically in relation to 3C within Agile teams.

To address this gap, we systematically explore how AI technologies, roles and functions support each aspect of 3Cs in Agile teamwork [10]. The 3Cs are *communication - involving the exchange of information among team members; collaboration - focusing on joint problem-solving and shared decision-making; and coordination - ensuring the effective management of interdependent tasks.*

3 Research Methodology

This section presents the research methodology, based on the guidelines outlined by Petersen et al. [11], for conducting a systematic mapping study.

3.1 Research Questions

The primary objective of this SMS is to provide a comprehensive overview of research conducted on AI in the context of teamwork within Agile software development. To achieve this, the study is guided by the main research question: *What is the research conducted on Artificial Intelligence in Agile teamwork?*

To further refine the scope, we define key research questions (RQs) as follows:

RQ1. *What is the temporal distribution of studies?* Understanding the distribution of studies to identify patterns and trends over time.

RQ2. *What are the key characteristics of the studies?* Examining the dissemination of research across venues, analyzing the nature of the studies, and categorizing the research methods to identify different approaches.

RQ3. *What aspects of Agile teamwork are investigated in these studies?* Classifying studies within the 3C model for structured analysis of research.

RQ4. *What AI technologies and roles are explored in the studies?* Investigating the roles and functions that AI technologies played in Agile teamwork.

3.2 Search Protocol

The search process followed a systematic approach using a search string formulated based on the PICO (Population, Intervention, Comparison, and Outcomes) framework [11]. The search string was iteratively refined to incorporate synonyms and variations to provide comprehensive coverage of relevant terminologies used by practitioners and researchers [12,13]. We used the following comprehensive query string to retrieve studies:

("agile" OR "extreme programming" OR "xp" OR "kanban" OR "lean" OR "scrum" OR "crystal" OR "dsdm" OR "fdd" OR ("feature" AND "driven" AND "development") OR "pair programming" OR "pp" OR "pair-programming")
AND ("software" OR "development" OR "software engineering")
AND ("artificial intelligence" OR "AI" OR "large language model" OR "LLM" OR "machine learning" OR "ML" OR "ChatGPT" OR "deep learning" OR "natural language processing" OR "NLP")
AND ("team" OR "teams" OR "teamwork")

3.3 Screening of Papers

Figure 1 provides an overview of screening process, illustrating the number of papers retrieved, screened, and excluded at each stage. The search was conducted in three digital libraries, retrieving 462 papers (ACM: 28, IEEE Xplore: 85, Scopus: 349). These libraries were selected for their comprehensive coverage of studies in computer science and software engineering. IEEE Xplore and ACM Digital Library were selected due to their significant role in publishing high-quality research in the field. Additionally, Scopus was included to ensure a diverse range of sources and broaden the scope of our search.

Table 1 presents the inclusion and exclusion criteria used in this study. We selected the timeframe (Jan 2001–Jan 2025) for data extraction, as 2001 marks the formal introduction of Agile software development. Since then, Agile methods have continuously evolved, shaping software development. Given the increasing integration of AI into Agile practices in recent years, this timeframe enables a comprehensive analysis of the research area of AI in relation to Agile teamwork over time. To minimize potential bias, the second author independently and randomly selected the papers for initial inclusion. Any uncertainties or disagreements were resolved through discussion and consensus. As a result, 20 studies were selected for detailed analysis.

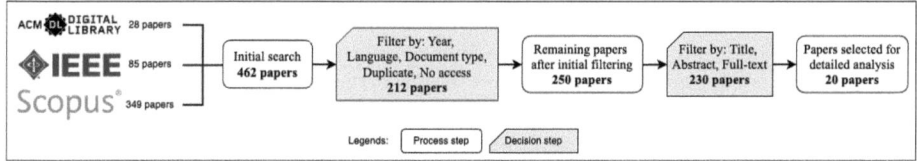

Fig. 1. Number of included studies during screening of papers.

Table 1. Inclusion and exclusion criteria.

Screening	ID	Criteria
Inclusion	IC1	Published between January 2001 and January 2025 inclusive
	IC2	Only English
	IC3	Published in conference, journal or magazine
	IC4	Studies with primary focus on Agile teamwork and AI for Agile
Exclusion	EC1	Published in workshop report, book, SLR, and SMS
	EC2	Duplicate papers
	EC3	No access to full text
	EC4	Studies not related to Agile Software Development
	EC5	Studies not related to Agile teamwork
	EC6	Studies focused on AI research (Agile for AI)
	EC7	Studies without AI

3.4 Keywording

In the next phase, we analyzed the abstracts and full texts of the selected papers to answer the research questions. A data extraction sheet was created to systematically collect relevant information from the studies. The collected data, including summarized results, can be accessed through the online repository[1].

4 Results

Answer to RQ1. Figure 2a shows the distribution of the 20 papers from 2018 to 2025. Notably, the papers from 2025 include only those published in January. Despite the inclusion criteria spanning from 2001, no papers were found prior to 2018, suggesting that research in this area has become prevalent in recent years.

Answer to RQ2. Figure 2a also shows that the majority of the selected studies are conference papers, with only three journal articles published from 2024 onwards. This indicates that research in this area is still in its early stages. To further classify the empirical studies, we adhered to the empirical standards of software engineering [14]. Figure 2b shows the empirical studies, which include

---

[1] 10.5281/zenodo.15543234

engineering research, experiments, action research, and data science methodologies. Among these, engineering research–focused on the proposal, development, and evaluation of technological artifacts–emerged as the most prevalent methodology. Most studies categorized as engineering research used experimental methods, case studies, or quantitative simulations to evaluate technological solutions.

Answer to RQ3. Figure 3 shows the distribution of studies across the 3C aspects of teamwork: collaboration, communication and coordination. Eight studies focus on coordination, while six each address collaboration and communication. These studies explore how AI supports various teamwork functions: in coordination, AI optimizes task allocation, improves effort estimation, and support project management; in collaboration, it enhances pair programming, decision-making, and documentation; and in communication, AI facilitates team meetings and analyzes team sentiment.

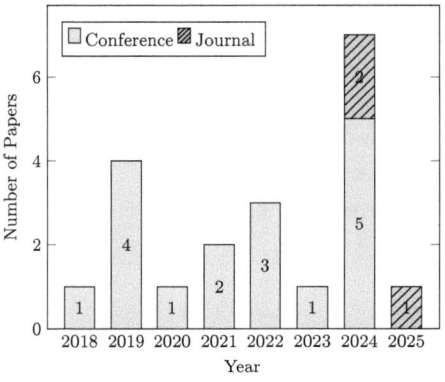
(a) By year and publication venue.

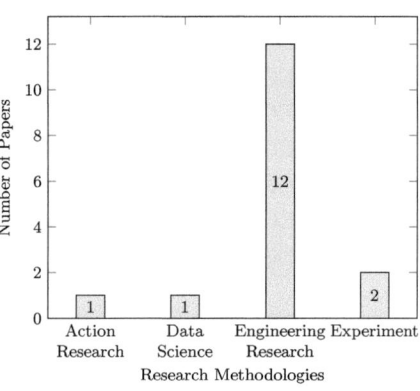
(b) By empirical research methodologies.

Fig. 2. Distribution of publication trends and research methodologies.

Answer to RQ4. To classify AI technologies and their corresponding roles, we adopted the classification presented by Mukhamediev et al. [13], with large language models (LLM) added as an additional category due to recent advancements in the field. Figure 3 shows that natural language processing (NLP) is the most dominant technology, followed by machine learning (ML). The findings suggest an evolution from classic AI techniques, such as NLP and ML algorithms, towards more advanced technologies like LLM. In terms of AI roles, most studies focus on applications with lower levels of autonomy, such as models and tools, while relatively few explore higher autonomy roles like agents, assistants, and bots. This distribution aligns with the AI functions shown in Fig. 4, based on the NIST taxonomy of AI use [15]. The most common AI function is recommendation, followed by process automation, detection, and monitoring. These functions primarily operate at the task level and therefore tend to require lower autonomy AI.

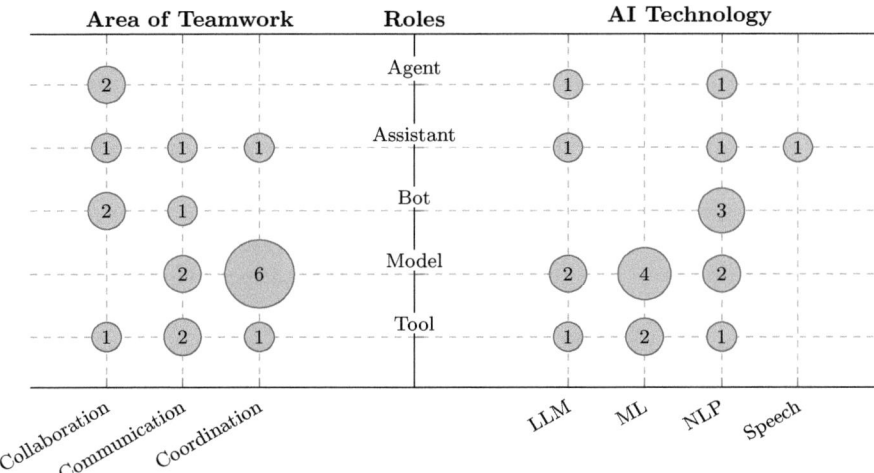

Fig. 3. Distribution of Agile teamwork and AI technologies with AI roles.

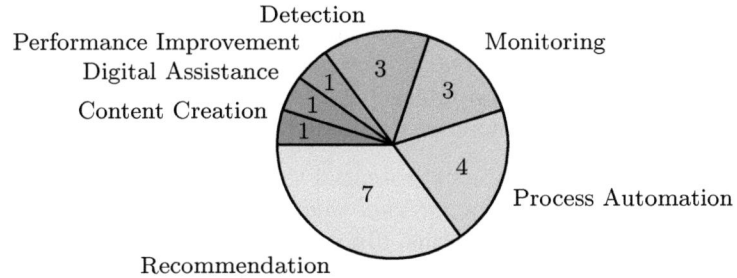

Fig. 4. Distribution of AI functions.

5 Current Research Gaps in AI and Agile Teamwork

This section presents the key learning points of the study, summarizes the research gaps, and discusses future implications.

Evolution of AI Research in Agile Teamwork. The findings of this study indicate significant growth in research in the integration of AI into Agile teamwork (as shown in Fig. 2a). However, the field remains in an exploratory phase, with most studies published in conferences and largely driven by empirical engineering research (as shown in Fig. 2b). This shows that there is an active search for practical solution and to determine if the solution is meaningful. A notable gap exists in non-empirical research that consolidates the practical knowledge and explores conceptual models for the integration of AI-driven tools and frameworks designed specifically for Agile practices.

Exploration of AI Technologies. This study finds that NLP is the predominant technology explored in the research (as shown in Fig. 3). Despite its potential to support complex problem-solving, enhance creativity, and assist in decision-making, LLM remains underexplored compared to NLP and ML. More research could examine how LLMs could enhance teamwork in Agile teams. In addition, while the trend of AI technology shifts from classic AI like NLP to more advanced AI like LLM, majority of the use cases continue to involve language-based approaches like tasks allocation, sentiment analysis and requirement analysis. As human aspects in Agile teamwork compose of more than just language, there are promising opportunities to explore further into other modalities of AI, such as images and videos, to enhance team dynamics.

AI Roles in Agile Teamwork. Based on the findings, the distribution of studies in the three aspects of teamwork is relatively equal, with team coordination taking a slightly larger proportion (as shown in Fig. 3). In relation to AI roles, majority of the studies on team communication and coordination explore lower autonomy AI while those of team collaboration have a slight focus on higher autonomy roles. The general emphasis on lower autonomy AI roles shows that the research field is in the risk-aware phase. AI which takes on a higher autonomy role would introduce concerns related to trust and control, which is yet to be well understood in Agile teams. Further research could study the impact of higher autonomy AI on team interactions and how AI might transition from being a mere tool to an autonomous agent that actively supports teamwork.

Threats to Validity. To mitigate potential threats and biases, we adhered to Wohlin et al. [16] guidelines. For *internal validity*, we followed the strategy outlined in Sect. 3 to define search terms, libraries, and inclusion-exclusion criteria. A key challenge was the lack of explicit use of 3C terminology in teamwork-related research, particularly regarding team coordination. To address this, relevant studies were inferred, and a clear definition of the 3C dimensions was established. Additionally, various digital libraries were used to ensure a comprehensive and inclusive collection of research studies. In cases of ambiguity, both authors collaboratively reviewed the studies to reach a consensus, ensuring consistency in study selection. To minimize bias in data extraction and synthesis regarding *conclusion validity*, both authors independently reviewed and cross-validated the extracted data. Any disagreements were resolved through discussion to ensure the reliability and accuracy of the findings.

6 Conclusion

This study provides a systematic overview of research on the integration of AI into teamwork within Agile software development, focusing on the 3Cs: communication, collaboration, and coordination. The results indicate that the research field is in an early exploratory phase to integrate AI into teamwork. While the existing studies are relatively balanced across the three aspects, language-based technologies–particularly natural language processing–are the most commonly explored. In contrast, large language models remain underexplored. Similarly, most studies focus on AI roles with lower levels of autonomy, such as tools and models, while higher-autonomy roles like agents and assistants have not been widely examined. These findings present research gaps and opportunities for future work to broaden the scope of AI applications and explore how more advanced, autonomous technologies can support and enhance Agile teamwork.

Acknowledgement. Special thanks to Professor Xiaofeng Wang for her unwavering guidance and insightful feedback on this research process.

References

1. Hoda, R., Salleh, N., Grundy, J.: The rise and evolution of agile software development. IEEE Softw. **35**(5), 58–63 (2018)
2. Tripp, J.F., Armstrong, D.J.: Exploring the relationship between organizational adoption motives and the tailoring of agile methods. In: 2014 47th Hawaii International Conference on System Sciences, pp. 4799–4806 (2014)
3. Beck, K., Beedle, M., et al.: Manifesto for agile software development (2001)
4. Barros, L., Tam, C., Varajao, J.: Agile software development projects–unveiling the human-related critical success factors. Inf. Softw. Technol. **170** (2024)
5. Das, S., Balmiki, A.K., Giri, N.C.: Artificial intelligence enables agile software development life cycle. Agile Softw. Dev. Trends Challenges Appl., 325–343 (2023)
6. Dam, H.K., Tran, T., et al.: Towards effective AI-powered agile project management. In: 2019 IEEE/ACM 41st Intl. Conf. on Software Engineering: New Ideas and Emerging Results (ICSE-NIER), pp. 41–44 (2019)
7. Perkusich, M., e Silva, L.C., et al.: Intelligent software engineering in the context of agile software development: a systematic literature review. Inf. Softw. Technol. **119**, 106241 (2020)
8. Peras, D., Stapić, Z., Matijević, M.: AI techniques and tools in agile software development: Preliminary research. In: Central European Conference on Information and Intelligent Systems, pp. 501–508 (2023)
9. Strode, D., Dingsøyr, T., Lindsjorn, Y.: A teamwork effectiveness model for agile software development. Empir. Softw. Eng. **27**(2), 56 (2022)
10. Sharp, H., Robinson, H.: Three 'c's of agile practice: collaboration, co-ordination and communication. In: Agile Software Development: Current Research and Future Directions, pp. 61–85 (2010)
11. Petersen, K., Vakkalanka, S., Kuzniarz, L.: Guidelines for conducting systematic mapping studies in software engineering: an update. Inf. Softw. Technol. **64**, 1–18 (2015)
12. Dybå, T., Dingsøyr, T.: Empirical studies of agile software development: a systematic review. Inf. Softw. Technol. **50**, 833–859 (2008)
13. Mukhamediev, R.I., Popova, Y., et al.: Review of artificial intelligence and machine learning technologies: classification, restrictions, opportunities and challenges. Mathematics **10**(15) (2022)
14. Ralph, P., bin Ali, N., et al.: Empirical standards for software engineering research (2021)
15. Theofanos, M., Choong, Y.Y., Jensen, T.: AI Use Taxonomy (2024)
16. Wohlin, C., Runeson, P., et al.: Experimentation in software engineering (2012)

Open Access This chapter is licensed under the terms of the Creative Commons Attribution 4.0 International License (http://creativecommons.org/licenses/by/4.0/), which permits use, sharing, adaptation, distribution and reproduction in any medium or format, as long as you give appropriate credit to the original author(s) and the source, provide a link to the Creative Commons license and indicate if changes were made.

The images or other third party material in this chapter are included in the chapter's Creative Commons license, unless indicated otherwise in a credit line to the material. If material is not included in the chapter's Creative Commons license and your intended use is not permitted by statutory regulation or exceeds the permitted use, you will need to obtain permission directly from the copyright holder.

NLP and GenAI in Agile Project Management: A Systematic Mapping Study

Daniel Planötscher[✉][iD]

Free University of Bolzano, NOI Techpark - via Bruno Buozzi, 1, 39100 Bolzano, Italy
`dplanoetscher@unibz.it`

Abstract. With the widespread adoption of generative AI, the field of Natural Language Processing (NLP) is witnessing the emergence of a new era. Historically, NLP has already been shown to have a diverse range of potential use cases within the field of Agile Project Management (APM). Hence, increasing amounts of research are exploring the use of NLP in APM. Through a systematic mapping study, this paper explores the research landscape of applying NLP technologies, including LLMs, to the various activities and practices of APM. It has been found that mostly planning activities have been explored for applying NLP, suggesting that future research may need to explore the use of NLP in other activities of agile project management. Furthermore, research in this field commonly utilizes traditional NLP methods, with notable attention also given to newer LLM technologies, such as generative AI.

Keywords: Agile Project Management · NLP · Natural Language Processing · Generative AI · Mapping Study

1 Introduction

After agile software development has taken over the industry in the last few decades [1], project management activities are also increasingly moving towards agile values, embracing adaptation to change and shorter delivery cycles. However, with this shift, new issues have emerged, such as changing requirements and mismatching estimations [9]. Several studies have suggested the use of NLP, as well as generative AI, for addressing these newly emerged pain points. With the widespread adoption of generative AI, the field of NLP is experiencing a new dawn [7], as generative AI introduces previously unattainable capabilities into the field of NLP.

The objective of this paper is to provide an overview of the current research landscape of the application of NLP and LLMs in agile project management through a Systematic Mapping Study (SMS). In addition, research gaps in this subject area will be explored, leading to opportunities for future research.

2 Related Work

Even though NLP and generative AI have gained popularity in recent years, only a few secondary studies have investigated their current applications in agile project management practices.

Raharjana et al. [14] focused on investigating different applications of NLP for user stories. The study highlighted the use of NLP for defect discovery and model generation. Similarly, Manrique-Losada et al. [11] presented a systematic literature mapping, showing the application of NLP in managing and processing requirements and user stories. The study identified various NLP techniques to classify, extract and analyze user stories. Additionally, Mehraj et al. [12] examined the application of AI in requirements engineering, considering its uses and the challenges linked to it.

However, the purpose of this SMS is to provide an overview of the field of agile project management as a whole and how NLP is used in it.

3 Research Method

The research method chosen for this study is a systematic mapping study, following the guidelines of Kitchenham and Chartes [10]. For this, the following research questions were developed:

1. RQ1: What are the temporal trends in the research landscape of NLP applications within agile project management?
2. RQ2: How is NLP being utilized in the various phases of agile project management?
3. RQ3: What are the predominant NLP technologies and techniques employed in agile project management, and what are their specific applications?

Using these questions, the inclusion and exclusion criteria were established. For the inclusion criterion, a guiding sentence was defined: *Studies must focus specifically on the application and impact of natural language processing within the context of agile project management.* From this, the following exclusion criteria were derived:

1. Study is not an article, conference paper, or academic journal.
2. Study is not in English.
3. Study does not show applications of natural language processing/LLMs/ generative AI.
4. Study is not specifically for agile software development.
5. Study does not focus on any software project management practice (e.g., requirements engineering, project planning).
6. Study is a secondary study (systematic literature review or mapping study).
7. Study has a similar study from the same authors, that was already selected (e.g. it is a preceding or succeeding study).

With this, a variety of keywords and synonyms were devised:

- **Agile (Software Development)**
  - *Synonyms:* Kanban, Scrum, Lean, Extreme Programming, XP, Scaled Agile Framework
- **Natural Language Processing/Generative AI**
  - *Synonyms:* Generative Artificial Intelligence, GPT, LLM, Language Model, AI-generated, AI-driven, Prompt Engineering, NLP
- **Project Management**
  - *Synonyms:* Requirements Engineering, Requirements Analysis, Requirements Specification, Requirements Elicitation, Requirements Management, Project Planning, Project Scheduling, Project Coordination, User Story, Software Requirements, Artefact, Meeting

For conducting the search, the following digital libraries were chosen: Scopus, IEEE Xplore and Scopus (Preprints). Scopus (Preprints) was selected, as the investigated field is still only emerging, and therefore, many papers in this field are only available as preprints. A total of 286 papers were collected for this study. After the selection process, 102 studies were finally selected for this study (see Table 1). The full list of selected papers is available in [13].

Table 1. Papers selected and excluded from this study

Digital Library	Initial amount	After duplicate removal	After final selection
Scopus	138	136	76
IEEE	122	78	17
Scopus (Preprints)	26	13	9
Total	286	227	102

For each paper, the following data was extracted:

- **Publication year:** Used for analyzing the temporal evolution of the research area.
- **Use case:** Used to extract the use cases of NLP from the study, such as backlog refinement, requirements specification, etc. Since some studies proposed multiple use cases, a total of 124 use cases were identified.
- **Agile activity:** For each use case, the agile activity in which it is most likely applied was derived. The activities are: *Initiation* (understanding project's vision and goals, as well as gathering requirements), *Planning* (defining requirements and time plans), *Implementation* (development of the project), *Review/Retrospectives* (assessing progress), and *Cross-Phase* (use case applies to more phases).
- **Technology used:** For each use case, also the technology used was extracted. The technologies were categorized into 3 groups: *traditional NLP* (e.g., TF-IDF, n-gram models, Named Entity Recognition, ...), *small LLMs* (e.g.,

BERT, RoBERTa, or other models with typically <1B parameters), and *generative AI models* (e.g., GPT, LLaMA, ...). This categorization was chosen due to the significant differences in capabilities and applications of the three technology groups.

4 Results

4.1 RQ1: Evolution of the Research Landscape

After the first paper was published in 2010, the area remained relatively unexplored for the following years. However, from 2020 onward, the number of publications started to increase drastically, peaking in 2024, when over a third of all the publications in the field were published. This may be related to the introduction of generative AI models, such as GPT-3 in late 2020. Hence, the research activity in this area is currently at an all-time high, as this SMS was written in January 2025 (Fig. 1).

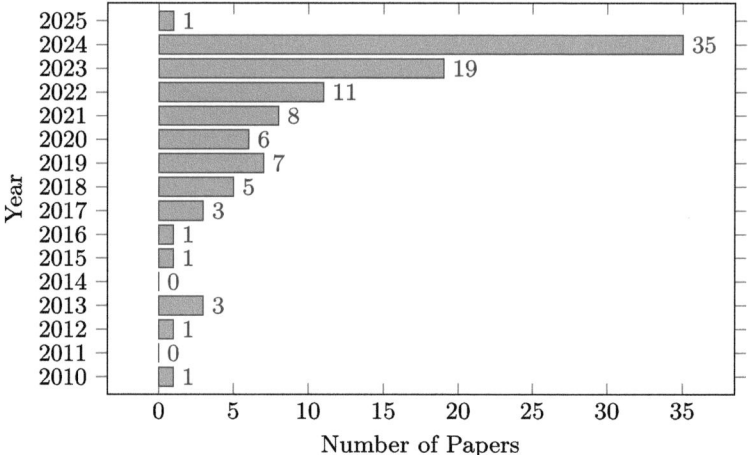

Fig. 1. Evolution of the Number of Papers Over Time

4.2 RQ2: Use Cases of NLP in Agile Project Management

Current research focuses mainly on the integration of NLP in *planning* activities of APM (Fig. 2), especially for working with requirements. Here, NLP is typically used for *modeling requirements* [6], such as the generation of UML diagrams (Fig. 3). Other applications of NLP in agile planning focus on tasks related to the *quality of requirements*, such as assessing their quality based on well-established criteria [16]. Also, the *management of non-functional requirements (NFR)* is being explored, for example by deriving them from user stories [2].

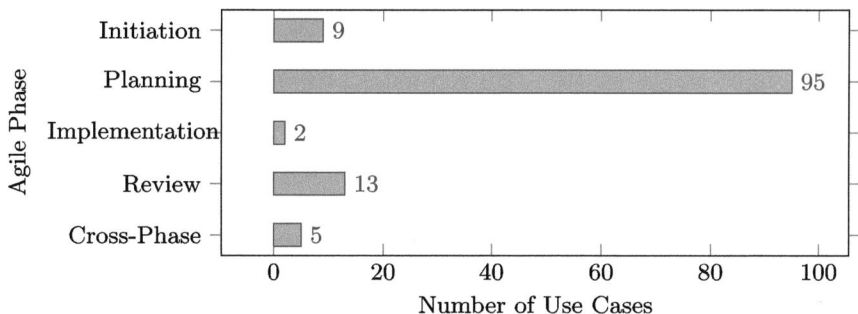

Fig. 2. Number of NLP Use Cases in Agile Project Management Phases

Other investigated use cases of NLP in APM are the *refinement of backlogs* (such as prioritization of requirements [15]) and *effort estimation* (for example, the derivation of T-Shirt sizes from user stories [4]).

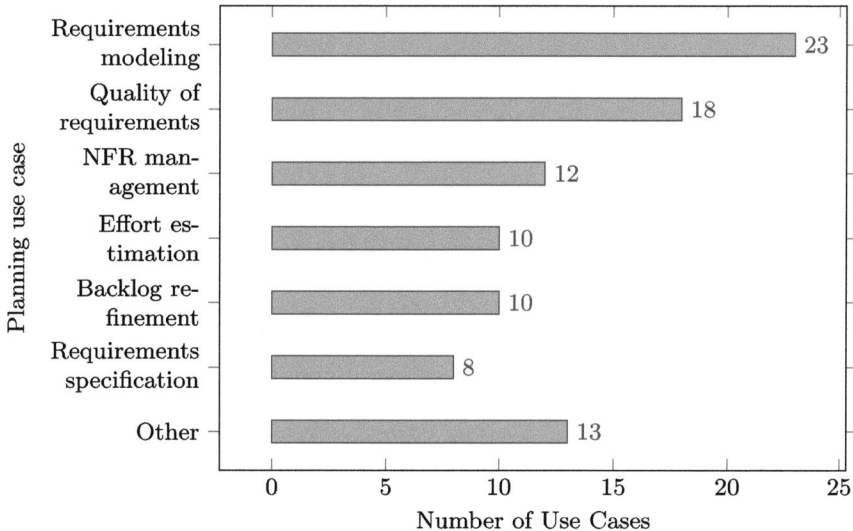

Fig. 3. Number of Use Cases for NLP in Agile Planning

In other phases, such as the *initiation* phase, NLP is used to develop goal models or to elicit requirements (3 studies each). Also notable is that some studies (3 papers) are exploring the potential of using these technologies to enhance agile meetings, such as daily scrums, feature refinement, and planning meetings [3].

For a complete list of the papers analyzed and the final categorizations of this SMS, refer to [13].

4.3 RQ3: Predominant NLP-Technologies in APM

Currently, most use cases (61) still rely on *traditional NLP techniques*. Here, oftentimes *POS-tagging* is used to comprehend sentence structures and to extract relevant information from user stories [6].

In addition, the usage of *small LLMs* was explored in 15 studies. Here, mainly *BERT-based models* are used to better understand natural language. By introducing contextual awareness, higher-quality output can be achieved at the cost of more computational needs. Smaller LLMs are used, for example, for better extraction of NFR from user stories, such as privacy requirements [8].

Nevertheless, an increasing number of publications have recently explored the potential of generative AI in APM. 43 use cases rely on generative AI models, such as GPT models, for more sophisticated tasks, such as automatically generating user stories [5].

5 Discussion

Another goal of this study is the derivation of potential gaps in current research and to provide opportunities for future studies. In general, only a few primary studies have explored use cases that may arise in phases besides the planning phase. This provides a potential gap for future studies that may focus on incorporating NLP and LLMs into later steps of the APM process.

It is interesting to point out that even though planning activities are explored in many studies, only a few papers have explored the initiation phase. Hence, another potential gap is the requirements elicitation and gathering phase, where requirements are collected from the stakeholders to understand the project's goals. This is important as it serves as a baseline for effective planning later on.

By further consolidating the data extracted in this SMS, the relationship between the APM activity and the NLP technology used can also be investigated. As depicted in Fig. 4, most studies investigated the usage of conventional NLP in planning activities. In this phase, the usage of LLM technologies is also comparatively high. The figure further demonstrates that the research on other phases is very limited.

6 Limitations

There are a few limitations and threats to the validity of the findings of this study. In general, the systematic mapping study was conducted by only one author. To counteract this issue, the study selection and data extraction was performed twice to ensure its accuracy.

Furthermore, some categories were designed to be slightly broad. This was decided to provide a broader overview over the whole research area, yet may lead to the loss of some detail in the analysis.

Additionally, this secondary study does not determine whether the proposals of each primary study were implemented or whether tools are provided to use

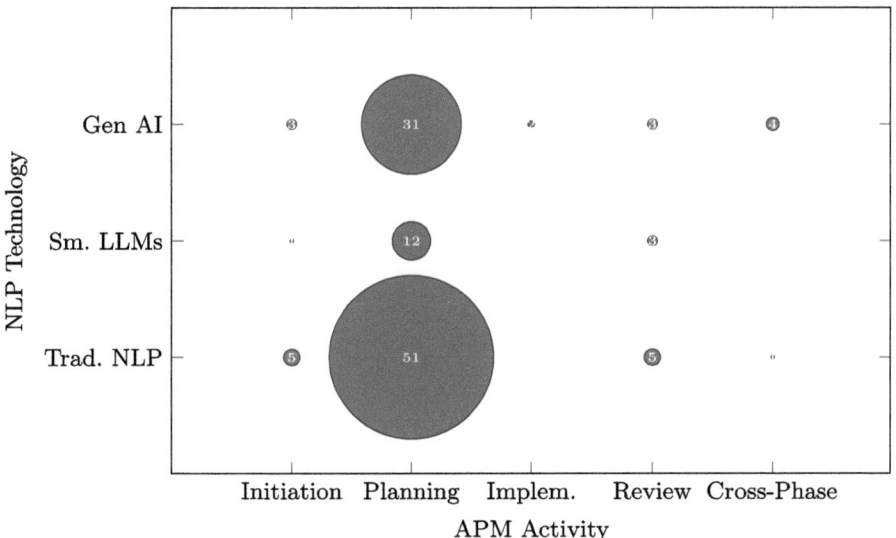

Fig. 4. Mapping - APM Activity vs NLP Technology

the results. This may have an impact on the applicability of the primary studies' results in the real world and might be interesting to explore in future work.

Lastly, it might be informative to investigate whether the developed tools operate fully autonomously or facilitate collaboration with AI, as this is a trending topic in the field of generative AI.

7 Conclusion

In conclusion, this systematic mapping study identified current trends in the emerging field of NLP applied to APM, by analyzing 102 publications. It provided a detailed analysis of the currently most researched use cases of NLP in APM. For now, the main focus was on the planning phases of agile project management. Here, NLP is especially used for enhancing requirements, e.g. by generating models or assessing the quality of requirements. In addition, it was found that most studies still rely on conventional NLP technologies. However, newer studies also explored the potential use of LLMs, such as GPT or BERT, for agile project management tasks.

Furthermore, this paper analyzed potential gaps in this field of study, specifically showing that other APM phases, besides the planning phase, such as the initiation phase, have only been the focus of a few studies.

Future secondary studies in this field could investigate whether the proposals of the primary studies have been implemented or provide software tools that practitioners can use. Furthermore, it could be investigated whether the tools provided also support collaboration on tasks with an LLM, as this is being proposed by an increasing number of studies in the field of generative AI.

References

1. State of Agile (2025). https://stateofagile.com. Accessed 20 Jan 2025
2. Ain, Q.U., Nisa, S.U., et al.: Beyond agile: NLP-driven quality attributes retrieval using ChatGPT in software development strategies. In: 2024 International Conference on Engineering & Computing Technologies (ICECT), pp. 1–6. IEEE (2024)
3. Cabrero-Daniel, B., Herda, T., Pichler, V., Eder, M.: Exploring human-AI collaboration in agile: Customised LLM meeting assistants. In: International Conference on Agile Software Development, pp. 163–178. Springer Nature Switzerland Cham (2024)
4. Catak, T., Durdu, P.O., Omurca, S.I.: Enhancing agile effort estimation: an NLP approach for software requirements analysis. In: 2024 International Congress on Human-Computer Interaction, Optimization and Robotic Applications (HORA), pp. 1–8. IEEE (2024)
5. Dos Santos, C.A., Bouchard, K., Petrillo, F.: AI-driven user story generation. In: 2024 International Conference on Artificial Intelligence, Computer, Data Sciences and Applications (ACDSA), pp. 1–6. IEEE (2024)
6. Elallaoui, M., Nafil, K., Touahni, R.: Automatic transformation of user stories into UML use case diagrams using NLP techniques. Procedia Comput. Sci. **130**, 42–49 (2018)
7. Hagos, D.H., Battle, R., Rawat, D.B.: Recent advances in generative AI and large language models: Current status, challenges, and perspectives. IEEE Transactions on Artificial Intelligence (2024)
8. Herwanto, G.B., Quirchmayr, G., Tjoa, A.M.: Leveraging NLP techniques for privacy requirements engineering in user stories. IEEE Access (2024)
9. Hoda, R., Murugesan, L.K.: Multi-level agile project management challenges: a self-organizing team perspective. J. Syst. Softw. **117**, 245–257 (2016)
10. Keele, S., et al.: Guidelines for performing systematic literature reviews in software engineering. Tech. rep., Technical report, ver. 2.3 EBSE technical report. EBSE (2007)
11. Manrique-Losada, B., Moreira, F., Cadavid, E.J.: NLP in requirements processing: a content analysis based systematic literature mapping. In: World Conference on Information Systems and Technologies, pp. 251–260. Springer (2024)
12. Mehraj, A., Zhang, Z., Systä, K.: A tertiary study on AI for requirements engineering. In: International Working Conference on Requirements Engineering: Foundation for Software Quality, pp. 159–177. Springer (2024)
13. Planötscher, D.: Results of the SMS (2025). https://docs.google.com/spreadsheets/d/1fzuLU4mGEPGmMxALEODVZJlUoqMZnXbENNGQ3rvMOvI/edit?gid=228570987#gid=228570987. Accessed 26 Feb 2025
14. Raharjana, I.K., Siahaan, D., Fatichah, C.: User stories and natural language processing: a systematic literature review. IEEE Access **9**, 53811–53826 (2021)
15. Sami, M., Rasheed, Z., Waseem, M., Zhang, Z., Herda, T., Abrahamsson, P.: Prioritizing software requirements using large language models (2024)
16. Wang, T., Wang, C., Li, T., Liu, Z., Zhai, Y.: User story quality assessment based on multi-dimensional perspective: a preliminary framework. In: iStar, pp. 7–13 (2022)

Open Access This chapter is licensed under the terms of the Creative Commons Attribution 4.0 International License (http://creativecommons.org/licenses/by/4.0/), which permits use, sharing, adaptation, distribution and reproduction in any medium or format, as long as you give appropriate credit to the original author(s) and the source, provide a link to the Creative Commons license and indicate if changes were made.

The images or other third party material in this chapter are included in the chapter's Creative Commons license, unless indicated otherwise in a credit line to the material. If material is not included in the chapter's Creative Commons license and your intended use is not permitted by statutory regulation or exceeds the permitted use, you will need to obtain permission directly from the copyright holder.

The Third International Workshop on Global and Hybrid Work in Software Engineering (GoHyb)

Hybrid Work in Agile Software Engineering: Current Research and Future Directions

Fateme Broomandi[1]([✉]), Maria Paasivaara[1], Emily Laue Christensen[1], Sonja Hyrynsalmi[1], and Dron Khanna[2]

[1] LUT University, Mukkulankatu 19, 15210 Lahti, Finland
{fateme.broomandi,maria.paasivaara}@lut.fi
[2] Wuerth Phoenix S.R.L., Via Johann Kravogl 4, 39100 Bolzano, Italy

Abstract. Hybrid work has become the new normal in post-pandemic software engineering. It is a timely topic that has attracted increasing attention among software engineering practitioners and researchers alike. In this paper, we summarize the findings from the third *International Workshop on Global and Hybrid Work in Software Engineering* (GoHyb) that was organized in conjunction with the XP 2025 conference. We present future research topics related to hybrid work in agile software engineering, which were brainstormed and collected during the workshop, supplemented with a systematic review of the literature on current and future research topics.

Keywords: Research directions · Hybrid work · Agile software engineering · Agile software development

1 Introduction

Hybrid work in agile software engineering, which combines work in and outside offices [6], appears to be here to stay. Despite the sudden shift to remote work during the Covid-19 pandemic, productivity in software engineering seemed to remain stable, with many employees reporting good or excellent performance [4,19], and we learned that remote work could provide flexibility and better work-life balance for employees [5,17].

Soon after the pandemic, software companies started their journey from full remote work, towards the 'new normal', by adopting flexible hybrid work policies [18]. While remote work has many benefits, as mentioned, research has shown that hybrid work environments can weaken face-to-face interactions, reducing the sense of belonging and team cohesion [10,21], which are vital factors for motivation, performance, and team resilience [20]. Some studies also claim that turnover rates increased, and job satisfaction decreased [14], with reduced commitment and work quality as a result [7].

Later, companies started implementing explicit hybrid work policies, e.g., requiring employees to visit the office two to three days per week [8,9,11,16].

Recently, several large software-intensive companies have been pushing more rigid in-office mandates, requiring employees to work four, or even five days per week at the office, which raises the question: Does this development indicate that hybrid work in software engineering is going to disappear in the future?

We believe the opposite. We expect hybrid work to remain and stabilize as the new norm for organizations in the software engineering industry. Companies will need to find a balanced setup that meets their needs, is profitable for the company, and attracts talented employees. However, achieving this requires both effort and research-based insights to help companies determine: 1) effective hybrid work practices, and 2) appropriate hybrid work policies tailored to their specific circumstances. To support companies in this process, the software engineering research community must further investigate these topics and deliver practical, evidence-based advice. This will enable companies to make informed decisions based on solid research rather than relying solely on gut feeling.

To support research efforts in hybrid work in agile software engineering and to build a community around the topic, we have organized three yearly workshops: *The International Workshop on Global and Hybrid Work in Software Engineering* (GoHyb). In this paper, we summarize the findings from the third edition of the GoHyb workshop (GoHyb 2025)[1], which was organized in conjunction with *The 26th International Conference on Agile Software Development* (XP 2025)[2]. We present topics for future research that were brainstormed and collected during the workshop, supplemented with a systematic review of the literature on current and future research topics.

2 Methodology

We integrate qualitative data from the GoHyb 2025 workshop with insights drawn from primary studies identified in a forthcoming systematic literature review (SLR) on hybrid work in agile software engineering [12]. The workshop captures researchers' and practitioners' views, while the identified academic studies are analyzed. Together, the insights captured highlight key themes and research gaps.

2.1 Workshop

We organized GoHyb 2025, which took place on the first day of XP 2025, on June 2nd, in Brugg, Switzerland. GoHyb 2025 was a half-day face-to-face workshop consisting of two parts. The first part featured six presentations by the 17 participants, who shared their practical experiences and research findings on hybrid work in software engineering. The main topics covered in these presentations included:

– Differences in software engineers' perceived productivity based on work style [2],

---

[1] GoHyb 2025: https://conf.researchr.org/home/xp-2025/gohyb-2025.
[2] XP 2025: https://conf.researchr.org/home/xp-2025.

- Experiences of novice programmers with hybrid versus in-person pair programming,
- The importance of shared team purposes in hybrid work environments,
- Factors influencing trust within hybrid software development teams [22],
- Burnout and resilience in software engineering.

The second part of the workshop began with a keynote by Hendrik Esser titled *The Evolution of Hybrid Work at Ericsson: Experiences, Learnings, and Challenges,* followed by an interactive session titled *Hybrid Work in Agile Software Development: What Should We Research Next? Creating a Research Agenda.* This interactive session aimed to brainstorm future research topics and was attended by 12 researchers and agile practitioners from around the world.

In the interactive session, we applied a modified version of the 1–2–4–All technique from the Liberating Structures framework [13], where step '4' was omitted, resulting in a streamlined '1–2–All' format. First, participants were asked to individually write down topics related to hybrid work in agile software engineering on sticky notes, specifically addressing the question *'What should we research next?'*. After a few minutes of individual reflection, the participants formed pairs to discuss, elaborate on, and expand their ideas. Finally, each pair presented their ideas to the whole group, one after another, until all contributions had been shared. We recorded the presentations of the pairs with their consent and used the transcriptions and the sticky notes as data sources for this research.

2.2 Systematic Literature Review

To complement the workshop findings, we analyzed the studies identified in our forthcoming SLR on hybrid work in agile software engineering [12]. The SLR focuses on peer-reviewed studies published in English between 2020 and 2025, which were conducted in professional agile software engineering settings with hybrid work. Primary studies were identified by combining searches carried out in five digital databases (IEEE Xplore, Scopus, ACM, SpringerLink, and ScienceDirect) in June and July 2025 with snowballing [15]. The query used in the databases combined three groups of keywords related to 'hybrid work', 'agile', and 'software engineering', respectively. After identification of 1185 records via the databases, subsequent screening for duplicates and relevance, and carrying out snowballing, 32 primary studies have been included to date (listed in Table 1).

As this paper focuses on research agendas, we chose the following three areas to explore in the primary studies: 1) investigated research topics, 2) research methodologies used, and 3) suggested research topics. Each primary study was coded using inductive thematic analysis to extract information about these three areas. This analysis provides a structured overview of existing literature and helps to contextualize the workshop results.

Table 1. List of primary studies

ID	Year	Authors	Title
P01	2021	Masood et al.	How New Zealand Software Companies Are Adapting Work Settings With Changing Times
P02	2022	Jackson et al.	Team Creativity in a Hybrid Software Development World
P03	2022	Neumann et al.	What Remains from Covid-19? Agile Software Development in Hybrid Work Organization
P04	2022	Sporesem and Moe	Coordination Strategies When Working from Anywhere
P05	2022	Sporesem et al.	Unscheduled Meetings in Hybrid Work
P06	2022	Tkalich et al.	What Happens to Psychological Safety When Going Remote?
P07	2022	Wang et al.	Co-Designing for a Hybrid Workplace Experience in Software Development
P08	2022	Šmite and Moe	Defining a Remote Work Policy: Aligning Actions and Intentions
P09	2022	Ågren et al.	Agile Software Development One Year into the COVID-19 Pandemic
P10	2022	Šmite et al.	Half-Empty Offices in Flexible Work Arrangements: Why are Employees Not Returning?
P11	2023	Bablo et al.	Overcoming Challenges of Virtual Scrum Teams: Lessons Learned Through an Action Research Study
P12	2023	Büyükgüzel and Balaman	The Spatial Organization of Hybrid Scrum Meetings: A Multimodal Conversation Analysis Study
P13	2023	Büyükgüzel and Mitchell	Progressivity in Hybrid Meetings: Daily Scrum as an Enabling Constraint for a Multi-Locational Software Development Team
P14	2023	Kemell and Saarikallio	Hybrid Work Practices and Strategies in Software Engineering - Emerging Software Developer Experiences
P15	2023	Tkalich et al.	Pair Programming Practiced in Hybrid Work
P16	2023	de Souza Santos et al.	Post-pandemic Resilience of Hybrid Software Teams
P17	2023	Moe et al.	Attractive Workplaces: What Are Engineers Looking for?
P18	2023	Jaspan and Green	Developer Productivity for Humans, Part 2: Hybrid Productivity
P19	2023	Smith et al.	Pandemic Asteroid Defense: DART Integration and Test in the time of COVID-19
P20	2023	Canedo et al.	Navigating Remote Work: Challenges and Adaptations of Agile Teams Amidst Covid-19
P21	2023	Liu et al.	Organizational Debt in Large-Scale Hybrid Agile Software Development: A Case Study on Coordination Mechanisms
P22	2023	Adil et al.	"Let's Discuss it in a Team Meeting!" Collaboration Challenges of Distributed Software Design
P23	2024	Moe et al.	Understanding the Difference between Office Presence and Co-presence in Team Member Interactions
P24	2024	Molléri et al.	Transformation to a Hybrid Workplace: A Case from the Norwegian Public Sector
P25	2024	Stray and Barbala	Slack Use in Large-Scale Agile Organizations: ESN Tools as Catalysts for Alignment?
P26	2024	Lisboa de Andrade et al.	Developing a Collaborative Recommendations Guide for Hybrid Software Development: A Focus Group Study
P27	2025	Šmite et al.	Dual Effects of Hybrid Working on Performance: More Work Hours or More Work Time
P28	2025	Stray et al.	Hybrid Meetings in Agile Software Development
P29	2025	Christensen et al.	Hybrid Work in Agile Software Development: Recurring Meetings
P30	2025	Christensen et al.	On the Evolution of Agile Software Team Work Arrangements
P31	2025	Hyrynsalmi et al.	Fostering a Sense of Belonging in Hybrid Work Within Agile Software Development
P32	2025	Zaidman et al.	Where is the Best Location to Conduct Scrum Meetings? A Quantitative and Qualitative Analysis of Developers' Perspectives

3 Workshop Outcomes: Suggested Topics for Future Research

Figure 1 presents each of the 49 topics suggested by academic and industry participants during the workshop. While some topics overlap, they collectively reflect a diverse range of concerns about the future of hybrid work in agile software engineering. Each topic is assigned an ID (T01, T02, etc.) for reference. We categorized suggested topics using socio-technical systems (STS) theory, which examines the interaction between social (human-centered) and technical (tools and processes) elements [1], a fitting framework since hybrid work and agile software engineering both rely on this interplay [3]. We classified the topics into four categories: 1) social, 2) technical, 3) interaction, and 4) education, which we explain in the following subsections. The topics were also analyzed and the themes and sub-themes identified are discussed further in Sect. 6.

Social topics:	Social and technology interaction topics:
T01 - Investigating motivations to return to the office	T25 - Balancing individual and team habits in hybrid work
T02 - Encouraging empathy and motivation for office return	T26 - Strategies for managing in-office days in hybrid work
T03 - Do employees really quit when forced back to office?	T27 - Challenges of in-office presence in distributed teams
T04 - Multitasking in hybrid meetings: distraction or efficiency booster?	T28 - Team collaboration across time zones in hybrid setups
T05 - How to foster a shared purpose in hybrid contexts?	T29 - How to decrease digital fatigue at hybrid work?
T06 - How to maintain the healthy tension for optimal performance in hybrid teams?	T30 - How to adapt agile methodology to hybrid work?
T07 - Understanding burnout among women in ICT hybrid work environments	T31 - Role of managers in hybrid work
	T32 - Hybrid interactions: how to define them? how to encourage strong and light hybrid interactions?
T08 - Does hybrid work increase stress for developers?	T33 - Sustaining hybrid work in agile software development: practices for long term
T09 - How do different sectors deal with hybrid work?	T34 - Role of the scrum master in hybrid agile teams
T10 - Organizational culture change in shift to hybrid work	T35 - Coordinating remote and on-site workers in hybrid environments
T11 - Why do so many developers prefer remote work?	
T12 - Demographic factors influencing work mode preferences	T36 - Integrating collaboration tools for better information visibility in hybrid work
T13 - Hybrid work experiences: comparing junior and senior employees	T37 - Does hybrid work complicate agile methodologies?
T14 - Impact of forced office presence on employee autonomy	T38 - Agile coaching in hybrid teams: challenges and adaptations
T15 - Autonomy in hybrid work: individual, team, and organizational perspectives	T39 - Tradeoffs in hybrid work: benefits, drawbacks, and mitigation strategies
T16 - How to motivate people to work in the office?	T40 - What to do during office days?
T17 - Decision making in hybrid work environments	T41 - Long term effects of hybrid work
	T42 - Investigating the impact of hybrid work on team performance
Technical topics:	
T18 - Are virtual offices viable substitutes for physical workspaces?	T43 - Optimizing retrospectives in hybrid agile teams
	T44 - Agile practices: what should be in-person or remote?
T19 - Algorithmic management in hybrid work: impacts and implications	T45 - Designing the optimal flow between home and office days in hybrid teams
T20 - Leveraging AI to optimize hybrid work environments	**Education topics:**
T21 - Developing a burnout detection tool for hybrid workers	T46 - How can we prepare students for the office first mode as they are pandemic sons?
T22 - Evaluating the effectiveness of digital collaboration tools in hybrid work	T47 - How to teach students to survive in hybrid work environments?
T23 - Digital infrastructure for sustainable hybrid work	T48 - How does education prepare for hybrid work?
T24 - Role of collaboration tools in hybrid work	T49 - Hybrid teaching in higher education: challenges and strategies

Fig. 1. Suggested topics by workshop participants.

Social topics focus on human aspects such as motivation, autonomy, well-being, retention, and team culture, highlighting the social dimension of hybrid work in agile software engineering.

Several social topics explore motivation to return to the office (T01, T02, T03), the balance between individual autonomy and organizational structure (T14, T15), and issues related to burnout and stress (T07, T08). Others emphasize maintaining healthy team dynamics and a strong organizational culture

(T05, T06, T10), while some address demographic and sector-specific factors that shape hybrid work experiences (T09, T12, T13). Additional topics focus on enhancing employee well-being and engagement (T03, T11, T16, T17). In total, 17 topics fall under the social category, representing approximately 35% of all suggestions, reflecting the strong emphasis participants placed on the human aspects of hybrid work in agile software engineering.

Technical topics center on tools, systems, infrastructure, and the role of technology in enabling or constraining hybrid work in agile software engineering. They highlight both the potential and limitations of technology in supporting hybrid work in agile software engineering environments. Some suggested topics in this category are the use of virtual offices as substitutes for physical spaces (T18), the influence of algorithmic management and AI-driven optimization (T19, T20), and the development of supportive tools such as burnout detection systems (T21). Other technical topics address the evaluation and improvement of digital collaboration tools and infrastructure (T22, T23, T24). In total, seven topics fall under the technical category, representing approximately 14% of all 49 topics. This shows that while technology is a critical enabler of hybrid work in agile software engineering, its role is specific and focused, complementing the social and interaction aspects rather than dominating them.

Social and technical interaction topics explore the relationship between people and technology, including collaboration practices, agile practices, and organizational adaptations. The interaction category reflects the coordination challenges at the core of hybrid work in agile software engineering, where individuals, processes, and tools must align across time and space. The topics address how individual and team habits evolve in hybrid environments (T25), strategies for managing office days and transitions between work modes (T26, T40, T45), and navigating distributed team presence (T27, T28). Several topics focus on agile practices, such as adapting methodologies (T30, T37), agile coaching (T38), and optimizing retrospectives (T43), as well as redefining roles like Scrum Master and managers (T31, T34). Other topics include collaboration between remote and on-site employees (T35), balancing interaction intensity (T32), and improving tool-supported visibility (T36). Broader concerns, such as sustaining hybrid work in agile software engineering (T33), evaluating long-term impacts (T41), and understanding trade-offs in performance and coordination (T39, T42, T44), underscore the evolving nature of hybrid work. With 21 topics in total, the interaction category represents approximately 43% of all suggestions, making it the most prominent area of interest among participants.

Education topics focus on preparing students and future professionals for hybrid work through education and training. We grouped these topics in their own category, to emphasize the role of academia in fostering hybrid work readiness. The four included topics (T46, T47, T48, T49) reflect growing recognition of the need to align educational practices with evolving work realities. Suggestions were provided about preparing students for hybrid work, teaching effective practices to survive in these environments, and supporting smoother transition from academia to industry. The education topic category represents approximately 8% of all 49 suggestions, highlighting a focused but important interest in equipping the next generation for hybrid work in agile software engineering.

4 Investigated Research Topics in Primary Studies

In the 32 primary studies (see Table 1) on hybrid work in agile software engineering identified through our SLR, thematic analysis revealed five major, interconnected themes, and multiple sub-themes, regarding the investigated topics. An overview of the themes and sub-themes is shown in Table 2. The recurrence of several themes within the same studies reflects the intertwined nature of organizational, technical, and human considerations in hybrid work within agile software engineering contexts.

Work setting and organizational adaptation, the most prominent theme (n = 18) reflects how organizations adjust structurally to hybrid work in agile software engineering environments. It includes work mode preferences and office presence (e.g., employee office presence and motivations for remote vs. office work), adaptations in daily work practices (e.g., modifying workflows, tools, and collaboration methods), and changes in work arrangements and policies (e.g., evolving company rules and flexible work guidelines).

Coordination, communication, and collaboration (n = 16) is the second most prominent theme, highlighting key challenges in hybrid work within agile software engineering and providing recommendations to address them. It focuses on collaboration and communication challenges, such as breakdowns, misalignment, and limited real-time interaction. Additionally, it covers meeting practices and challenges, where virtual meetings and asynchronous communication can reduce transparency and delay feedback.

The *people considerations* theme (n = 15) highlights how hybrid work impacts individuals, teams, and organizations on human and social levels. It covers how hybrid arrangements influence productivity and well-being, including focus and stress; employee motivation and retention, addressing engagement and job satisfaction; social connectedness, reflecting the need for informal bonding and cohesion; psychological safety and empowerment, focusing on employees' ability to speak up and feel autonomous; and creativity and innovation.

The *agile practice adaptation* theme (n = 8), explores how agile events, workflows, and team structures are modified for hybrid work. Adjustments to stand-ups, retrospectives, and sprint planning are common, along with increased reliance on digital tools. One key insight is that agile frameworks must evolve intentionally to balance structure and flexibility in hybrid settings.

Finally, the theme *technology and tools* (n = 4), while supported by a smaller set of studies, underpins many of the challenges and solutions discussed across the other themes. Tool adoption is critical for enabling teams in hybrid work arrangements to collaborate effectively, manage tasks transparently, and remain aligned. However, this topic is limited in the studies, compared to other topics, suggesting that technology alone is not enough to ensure agility.

Table 2. Overview of thematic analysis of topics investigated in the primary studies

Theme (n)	Sub-theme (n)	Evidence
Work setting and organizational adaptation (18)	Work mode preferences and presence (7)	P03, P08, P10, P14, P23, P27, P32
	Work practices adaptation in hybrid work (6)	P01, P09, P11, P24, P26, P30
	Work arrangements and policies (5)	P07, P08, P17, P26, P30
Coordination, communication and collaboration (16)	Collaboration and communication challenges and recommendations (8)	P04, P09, P11, P20, P21, P22, P23, P25
	Meeting practices and challenges (8)	P04, P05, P09, P12, P13, P28, P29, P32
People considerations (15)	Productivity and well-being (5)	P09, P11, P18, P20, P27,
	Employee motivation and retention (4)	P09, P10, P14, P17
	Social connectedness (3)	P09, P16, P31
	Psychological safety and empowerment (2)	P06, P09
	Creativity and innovation (1)	P02
Agile practice adaptation (8)	Agile practices in hybrid work (8)	P03, P09, P11, P15, P19, P20, P29, P32
Technology and tools (4)	Tool usage and adoption (4)	P09, P19, P20, P25

5 Research Methodologies in Primary Studies

This section examines the research methodologies employed in the 32 primary studies (see Table 1) identified through our SLR. An overview of the research designs used in the studies is shown in Fig. 2, while the employed data collection methods are shown in Fig. 3. More detailed information about the research designs and data collection methods is made available in the supplementary materials[3].

---

[3] Supplementary materials: https://doi.org/10.6084/m9.figshare.29433200.v1.

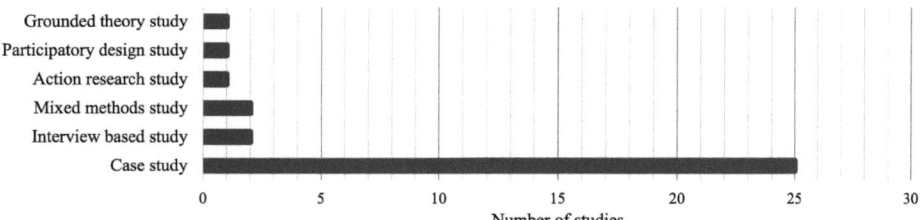

Fig. 2. Research designs used in the primary studies.

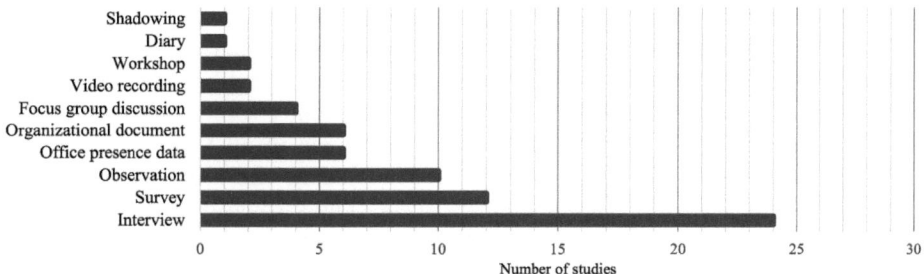

Fig. 3. Data collection methods used in the primary studies.

As shown in Fig. 2, the majority of primary studies (25 studies) adopted a case study research design, which are useful for providing in-depth insights into the evolving nature of hybrid work in agile software engineering. The dominance of case studies suggests a need for deep, contextualized insights into how hybrid work is implemented and experienced in agile software engineering environments. Interestingly, longitudinal case studies (P06, P08, P17, P18, P26, P30) provided valuable perspectives on temporal changes, such as shifts in team dynamics and employee motivations over time, highlighting the dynamic nature of hybrid work, rather than treating it as a static configuration.

Two studies were interview-based and two utilized mixed methods, where participants were not drawn from a specific case context. This highlights opportunities to diversify research designs and complement qualitative insights with quantitative or experimental approaches. Research designs such as action research, participatory design, and grounded theory were rarely used, but offer valuable and underexplored perspectives. For example, the lone study utilizing participatory co-design (P07) points to a gap in this approach. Similarly, grounded theory (P16), used in just one study, holds strong potential for developing theory as hybrid practices evolve.

As shown in Fig. 3, while the studies employed a diverse range of data collection methods, there was a strong reliance on interviews (24 studies) and surveys (12 studies). These methods effectively capture subjective experiences, but can potentially introduce self-reporting bias and limit insight into actual behaviors. Some studies incorporated contextual data through observation and shadowing, which is crucial to gain an understanding of how hybrid work is truly carried out. Notably, few studies collected data through video recordings (P12, P13) or diary entries (P18). These methods could offer deeper insights into day-to-day decision-making, stress patterns, or collaboration rhythms, which are particularly important for examining factors like digital fatigue or autonomy.

6 Future Research Directions

An overview of themes and sub-themes identified in the suggested research topics of the 32 studies, and in the topics suggested by the workshop (WS) participants is shown in Table 3. The themes and sub-themes identified in the suggested topics, in both the studies and the workshop (shown in Table 3) are largely consistent with those identified in the investigated study topics (see Table 2).

The relative frequency distribution of each theme in all three sources, i.e., topics investigated in the studies, topics suggested in the studies, and topics suggested in the workshop, are shown in Fig. 4. The strongest theme across all sources, *work setting and organizational adaptation*, emerges as the most prominent in the investigated study topics (29.5%), suggested study topics (37.1%), and workshop data (26.3%). Notably, the topics proposed in both the primary studies and the workshop closely mirror those already investigated, indicating a shared understanding of the critical role structural and cultural adjustments play in hybrid work. A consistent trend across all sources is the growing emphasis on formalizing hybrid work policies and refining day-to-day practices, highlighting this area as an increasingly central research priority.

People considerations are prominent as suggested topics in both the studies and the workshop. While the investigated topics in the studies show moderate attention to this area (24.6%), suggested study (27.1%) and workshop topics (29.9%) emphasize it even more. Sub-themes, such as productivity and well-being, motivation, and retention, were particularly discussed in the workshop, highlighting a strong focus on human factors in hybrid teams. This reflects a clear trend: a shift from focusing solely on structural changes like policies toward prioritizing employee experience, with a growing interest in sustaining engagement and well-being in hybrid work within agile software engineering environments.

The theme of *coordination, communication, and collaboration* receives notably less emphasis in suggested study topics compared to investigated ones, appearing in 26.2% of the investigated study topics, 20% of the suggested study topics, and only 14% of the topics suggested in the workshop. While communication issues are generally well understood, the decreasing trend might indicate that communication is increasingly seen as a familiar challenge in hybrid work within agile software engineering, while more attention is leaning toward adaptability and employee well-being as the more urgent priorities.

The *agile practice adaptation* theme is consistently represented across all sources, with a slight decrease from investigated to suggested topics. The slightly lower representation of this theme, compared to the previously mentioned themes, indicates that while agile adaptation is ongoing, work setting

Table 3. Overview of thematic analysis of suggested topics in primary studies and workshop

Theme (Total, Studies, WS)	Sub-theme (Total, Studies, WS)	Evidence from studies and the workshop topics
Work setting and organizational adaptation (41, 26, 15)	Work arrangements and policies (13, 10, 3)	Studies: P01, P07, P08, P10, P17, P18, P24, P26, P29, P30 WS: T09, T10, T31
	Work practices adaptation in hybrid work (17, 10, 7)	Studies: P01, P03, P04, P07, P10, P16, P18, P22, P26, P30 WS: T04, T17, T26, T33, T40, T41, T45
	Work mode preferences and presence (11, 6, 5)	Studies: P03, P09, P10, P23, P29, P32 WS: T11, T12, T13, T27, T45
People considerations (36, 19, 17)	Productivity and well-being (13, 5, 8)	Studies: P07, P16, P18, P24, P27 WS: T06, T07, T08, T15, T21, T29, T42, T45
	Employee motivation and retention (9, 4, 5)	Studies: P03, P17, P20, P23 WS: T01, T02, T03, T14, T16
	Social connectedness (6, 4, 2)	Studies: P04, P09, P17, P31 WS: T05, T06
	Psychological safety and empowerment (5, 3, 2)	Studies: P06, P08, P09 WS: T14, T15
	Creativity and innovation (3, 3, 0)	Studies: P02, P07, P18
Coordination, communication and collaboration (22, 14, 8)	Collaboration and communication challenges and recommendations (13, 7, 6)	Studies: P04, P18, P21, P22, P23, P25, P30 WS: T25, T28, T32, T35, T36, T39
	Meeting practices and challenges (9, 7, 2)	Studies: P05, P12, P13, P18, P28, P29, P32 WS: T04, T43
Agile practice adaptation (12, 6, 6)	Agile practices in hybrid work (12, 6, 6)	Studies: P03, P14, P15, P20, P25, P32 WS: T30, T34, T37, T38, T43, T44
Technology and tools (12, 5, 7)	Tool usage and adoption (13, 6, 7)	Studies: P04, P05, P10, P12, P25 WS: T18, T19, T20, T22, T23, T24, T29
Educating students to hybrid work (4, 0, 4)	Education (4, 0, 4)	WS: T46, T47, T48, T49

and organizational adaptation, and people considerations, take the highest priority.

The *technology and tools* theme is mentioned across all sources but remains peripheral, with low representation overall. The focus is mainly on tool usage, reflecting their role as enablers of hybrid work rather than central research topics. However, with the rise of AI, topics suggested, particularly in the workshop, highlight the potential of AI-based tools for optimizing and managing hybrid

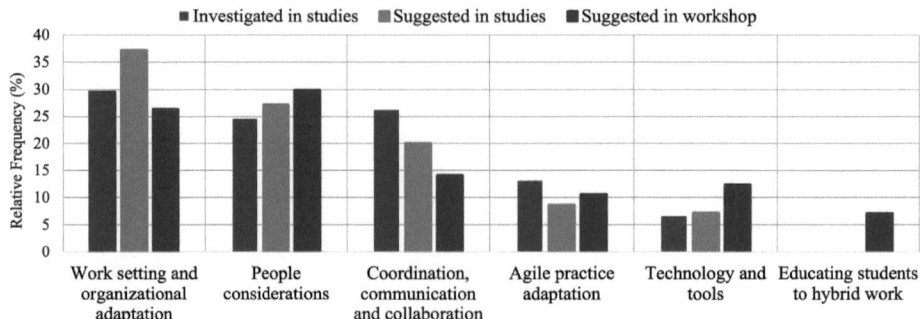

Fig. 4. Topic distribution across themes.

work, creating virtual offices, and detecting burnout, which suggests new and emerging areas of interest.

Finally, the theme *educating students to hybrid work* emerged only in the suggested topics from the workshop and is absent from the study topics. This highlights a forward-looking concern among workshop participants regarding training and education. The lack of instances of this theme could indicate a gap in academic discourse, presenting a potential opportunity for future research in hybrid work within agile software engineering. However, our SLR concentrates on hybrid work in professional environments; thus, this topic may be explored more in educational publications.

7 Final Remarks

The methodological landscape of the primary studies reveals a strong preference for empirical, context-specific investigations, particularly case studies, reflecting the complexity of hybrid work in agile software engineering environments and the importance of understanding these dynamics in the actual context. Grounded theory and longitudinal case studies are promising methodological approaches that would benefit from more attention. Longitudinal studies are particularly valuable, as many workshop participants expressed concern about the long-term impacts of hybrid work in agile software engineering. Grounded theory, on the other hand, is well-suited for exploring areas where existing theories fall short or are still emerging. Given that hybrid work in agile software engineering is a relatively new and evolving phenomenon, grounded theory allows researchers to build new conceptual frameworks directly from the lived experiences of practitioners. Moreover, there is a heavy reliance on interviews and surveys, which effectively capture subjective experiences. Future research could however benefit from adopting more objective data collection methods, as well as combining different methods, to provide a richer, more balanced, and broader understanding of hybrid work in the context of agile software engineering.

From a topic viewpoint, we can see that while, for example, communication has been extensively studied and is now considered a well-understood challenge, work setting and organizational adaptation issues continue to dominate research agendas. Despite this theme being investigated heavily in the studies, companies still struggle to define effective strategies and policies for hybrid work, suggesting that 'one size fits all' solutions are inadequate and that sector- or industry-specific studies are urgently needed, as also suggested in the workshop and the reviewed literature. Workshop topics also emphasize defining office presence, structuring office days to maximize value, clarifying the managerial role, and decision-making in hybrid work within the context of agile software engineering. Sub-themes under people considerations, such as motivation, retention, well-being, and productivity represent a growing trend in hybrid work research within agile software engineering. Meanwhile, academic preparation of students emerges as an important, yet under-researched area, highlighting critical gaps and opportunities for future exploration. In addition, the use of AI-based tools as enablers of hybrid work has great interest, as identified in the suggested workshop topics and in the literature.

However, the frequency of which a topic is mentioned, in the workshop or in literature, does not necessarily reflect its' importance or urgency. Some critical issues may be overlooked entirely, highlighting the need for researchers to prioritize practical significance, long-term impact, and contextual relevance.

Acknowledgement. We sincerely thank the Finnish Work Environment Fund for supporting this research through grant no. 240172. We also extend our gratitude to all the presenters and participants of the GoHyb 2025 workshop for their valuable contributions, ideas, and engaging discussions.

References

1. Abbas, R., Michael, K.: Socio-technical theory: a review. In: Papagiannidis, S. (ed.) TheoryHub book (2025). https://open.ncl.ac.uk, ISBN: 9781739604400
2. Aranda, G.N., Vizcaíno, A., Soto, J.P., Rolón, E., Garcés, K., García, F.O.: Are there any differences in the way that software engineers perceive their productivity depending on their work style? In: Post-conference proceedings of the International Conference on Agile Software Development, XP 2025 (2025)
3. Beck, K., et al.: Manifesto for agile software development (2001). http://agilemanifesto.org/. Accessed 26 June 2025
4. Bezerra, C.I., et al.: How human and organizational factors influence software teams productivity in COVID-19 pandemic: a Brazilian survey. In: Proceedings of the XXXIV Brazilian Symposium on Software Engineering, pp. 606–615 (2020)
5. Butler, J., Jaffe, S.: Challenges and gratitude: a diary study of software engineers working from home during COVID-19 pandemic. In: 2021 IEEE/ACM 43rd International Conference on Software Engineering: Software Engineering in Practice (ICSE-SEIP), pp. 362–363. IEEE (2021)
6. Conboy, K., Moe, N.B., Stray, V., Gundelsby, J.H.: The future of hybrid software development: challenging current assumptions. IEEE Softw. **40**(02), 26–33 (2023)
7. Ebert, C., Hemel, U.: Technology trends 2023: the competence challenge. IEEE Softw. **40**(3), 20–28 (2023)

8. Elias, J.: Google is offering an on-campus hotel 'special' to help lure workers back to the office (2023). https://www.cnbc.com/2023/08/04/google-offers-on-campus-hotel-special-to-lure-workers-back-in.html. Accessed 26 June 2025
9. Elias, J.: Google to crack down on office attendance, asks remote workers to reconsider (2023). https://www.cnbc.com/2023/06/08/google-to-crack-down-on-hybrid-work-asks-remote-workers-to-reconsider.html. Accessed 26 June 2025
10. Hyrynsalmi, S.M., Broomandi, F., Salman, I., Paasivaara, M.: Fostering a sense of belonging in hybrid work within agile software development. In: International Conference on Agile Software Development, pp. 37–51. Springer, Cham (2025)
11. Jassy, A.: Message from CEO Andy Jassy: Strengthening our culture and teams (2024). https://www.aboutamazon.com/news/company-news/ceo-andy-jassy-latest-update-on-amazon-return-to-office-manager-team-ratio. Accessed 26 June 2025
12. Khanna°, D., Christensen°, E.L., Broomandi, F., Paasivaara, M., Advait, D.: Revisiting hybrid work in agile software engineering: A systematic literature review. (Work in progress)
13. Liberating Structures: 1-2-4-all (nd). https://www.liberatingstructures.com/1-1-2-4-all/. Accessed 02 June 2025
14. Moe, N.B., Stray, V., Šmite, D., Mikalsen, M.: Attractive workplaces: what are engineers looking for? IEEE Softw. **40**(5), 85–93 (2023)
15. Mourão, E., Kalinowski, M., Murta, L., Mendes, E., Wohlin, C.: Investigating the use of a hybrid search strategy for systematic reviews. In: 2017 ACM/IEEE International Symposium on Empirical Software Engineering and Measurement (ESEM), pp. 193–198 (2017)
16. Nicholas, K., Hull, D.: Elon musk tells tesla workers to return to the office or lose their jobs (2022). https://www.latimes.com/business/technology/story/2022-06-01/elon-musk-tells-tesla-workers-to-return-to-the-office-or-lose-their-jobs. Accessed 26 June 2025
17. Russo, D., Hanel, P.H., Altnickel, S., van Berkel, N.: Predictors of well-being and productivity among software professionals during the COVID-19 pandemic-a longitudinal study. Empir. Softw. Eng. **26**(4), 62 (2021)
18. Šmite, D., Moe, N.B., Hildrum, J., Gonzalez-Huerta, J., Mendez, D.: Work-from-home is here to stay: call for flexibility in post-pandemic work policies. J. Syst. Softw. **195**, 111552 (2023)
19. Šmite, D., Tkalich, A., Moe, N.B., Papatheocharous, E., Klotins, E., Buvik, M.P.: Changes in perceived productivity of software engineers during COVID-19 pandemic: the voice of evidence. J. Syst. Softw. **186**, 111197 (2022)
20. de Souza Santos, R., Adisaputri, G., Ralph, P.: Post-pandemic resilience of hybrid software teams. In: 2023 IEEE/ACM 16th International Conference on Cooperative and Human Aspects of Software Engineering (CHASE), pp. 1–12. IEEE (2023)
21. de Souza Santos, R., Magalhaes, C., Franca, C.: Hybrid work well-being: Software professionals finding equilibrium. IEEE Software (2024)
22. Tyagi, S., Masood, Z.: Understanding factors influencing trust in software development teams in hybrid work settings: an empirical investigation. In: Post-Conference Proceedings of the International Conference on Agile Software Development, XP 2025 (2025)

Open Access This chapter is licensed under the terms of the Creative Commons Attribution 4.0 International License (http://creativecommons.org/licenses/by/4.0/), which permits use, sharing, adaptation, distribution and reproduction in any medium or format, as long as you give appropriate credit to the original author(s) and the source, provide a link to the Creative Commons license and indicate if changes were made.

The images or other third party material in this chapter are included in the chapter's Creative Commons license, unless indicated otherwise in a credit line to the material. If material is not included in the chapter's Creative Commons license and your intended use is not permitted by statutory regulation or exceeds the permitted use, you will need to obtain permission directly from the copyright holder.

Are there any Differences in the Way that Software Engineers Perceive their Productivity Depending on their Work Style?

Gabriela Aranda[1], Aurora Vizcaíno[2(✉)], Juan Pablo Soto[3], Elvira Rolón[4], Kelly Garcés[5], and Félix O. García[2]

[1] Universidad Nacional del Comahue, Neuquén, Argentina
gabriela.aranda@fi.uncoma.edu.ar
[2] Universidad de Castilla-La Mancha, Ciudad Real, Spain
{aurora.vizcaino,felix.garcia}@uclm.es
[3] Universidad de Sonora, Hermosillo, Mexico
juanpablo.soto@unison.mx
[4] Universidad Autónoma de Tamaulipas, Tampico, México
erolon@docentes.uat.edu.mx
[5] Universidad de los Andes, Bogotá, Colombia
kj.garces971@uniandes.edu.co

Abstract. In the wake of the COVID-19 pandemic, remote working seemed here to stay. However, attempts to return to working in the office are currently being made, mainly by large multinationals. We therefore set out to investigate software-industry workers' opinions of their productivity in their current work mode. This paper presents the results of surveys applied to software engineers from Mexico, Spain, Colombia and Argentina with the purpose of analysing how they perceive their productivity and that of their team when working either partially or totally in a remote manner. The results indicate that most of the respondents prefer to work remotely. Furthermore, according to their perception, their productivity and that of their team is, in general, equal or superior to that achieved in the office.

Keywords: Remote work · productivity · office first

1 Introduction

Several individual work modes emerged after the pandemic, which have been classified by Šmite et al. in [1] as: office mode (always in the office); office-first (more time in the office than at home), office-remote mix (an approach that allows total flexibility), remote-first (involving more time working outside the office than in it) and remote mode (working from home every day). Despite this diversity, some large multinationals would prefer to return to the traditional mode with the aim of improving productivity and knowledge exchange and are consequently encouraging software engineers to return to their offices. Some examples are Amazon, Google, and Apple [2]. This paper analyses how engineers from four Spanish-speaking countries perceive their productivity as compared to when it was completely onsite. The respondents were divided into two groups: those who work only one or two days per week at home, who we refer to as office-first in accordance with Šmite et al.'s nomenclature, and those who work at home three or more days per week, considering remote-first and totally remote in the same group. This allowed us to analyse whether there is a difference between the opinions of the two groups.

2 Related Work

Several studies currently focus on software development teams' change in productivity before, during and after the COVID-19 pandemic. For example, in a pre-pandemic study [3], the relationship between happiness and productivity among software engineers and concluded that those who were happy developing software were also more productive, with a positive correlation between happiness and productivity. Later, in an investigation of the productivity and well-being of software engineers during the pandemic, found that anxiety, distractions, and lack of motivation began to increase during the early stages of remote work [4]. However, around the same time, a survey of software development teams in Brazil was conducted to identify productivity challenges. Using the responses of 58 participants from various regions as a basis, they found that 74.1% of the participants considered their productivity to be good or excellent, and 84.5% felt motivated and believed they had good communication with their colleagues [5].

In more recent works [6, 7], the authors conducting mining of public domain repositories in order to identify changes in developer activity metrics during and after the pandemic. One of the most relevant findings of this study was that the percentages of commits and issues in 2023 were lower than in 2020. However, further studies indicated that some people experienced difficulties with their well-being during remote work [1, 8]. Other recent works have suggested that purely remote work reduces creativity and consequently the productivity in software development companies [4, 9].

In [10], the authors conducted a survey to analyse how different factors influence performance when working remotely. The data were analysed using PLS-SEM, and the authors found direct negative effects of stress on performance and direct positive effects of motivation on performance, which align with numerous findings from social science research in contexts other than remote work. They additionally found that skills and experience, trust, communication, and knowledge sharing play important roles in remote work and affect employees' performance.

Given that the aforementioned studies do not indicate a single opinion about productivity, as this depends on the context and when they were conducted. Furthermore, most of the current studies have been carried out in Nordic countries owing to the prolific researchers residing there, this study, therefore, aims to analyse the perspective of employees from four Spanish-speaking countries (Spain, Colombia, Mexico, and Argentina), and compare the opinions about productivity between those who work in "remote and remote first" mode with that of those who work in the "office-first" mode.

3 Research Methodology

This study was carried out by conducting a survey using a questionnaire that initially consisted of questions regarding the participants' socio-demographic information and previous experience (age, country of origin, remote work experience, how many days they worked at home, etc.), followed by a second section focusing on their opinions about their productivity, knowledge sharing, motivation, etc. Due to space limitations, we will focus on those related to productivity.

The questions were designed on the basis of previous studies and surveys that dealt with similar topics [11] and a focus group conducted with 33 software industry workers. The survey was sent to the first participants on September 26, 2024, and they were given until October 31 of the same year to respond. The objective was to attain 100 responses per country, with Mexico being the only one to exceed that number. Despite not meeting that goal, the number of responses obtained from the other countries was considered sufficient to analyse trends in the results.

Some responses were received from people who had not worked onsite for at least 2 years, despite the fact that this requirement was stated in the survey header, so these were discarded. Additionally, incomplete surveys were also removed, leaving the following: a total of 236 responses, 24 from Argentina, 89 from Mexico, 65 from Colombia, and 58 from Spain.

As indicated in the introduction, for the analysis of this study, only responses from residents of Argentina, Colombia, Spain, and Mexico were considered.

The responses from employees were subsequently divided into a remote + remote first group and a second group containing those who worked at home only one or two days (office first) (see Table 1). The responses of those who always worked in the office were discarded.

Table 1. Number of participants per country in each group

Remote first and Remote			
Argentina	Spain	Colombia	Mexico
18	41	60	78
Office first			
Argentina	Spain	Colombia	Mexico
6	17	5	11

Once the data was collected, we analyzed it from two points of view; firstly, a descriptive one (through visualizations) and then an inferential perspective to validate whether observed differences were statistically significant. We applied the Student's t-test to analyze differences between both groups.

4 Results

The following sections first show an analysis of the respondents' demographic characteristics, after which the results are presented.

4.1 Demographic Information

The majority of the respondents in the four countries were men, representing more than 67% of the sample. The highest proportion of female respondents was from Argentina (33%), while the lowest was from Colombia (12%). Spain and Mexico attained slightly higher values, with a female representation of around 20%. Only one respondent in the entire sample identified as non-binary. With regard to their years of experience working in software development companies, most respondents indicated they had less than 5 years of experience. Approximately 30% of the respondents in the four countries were in the 5 to 10 years range, while the 11 to 20 years range predominated in Spain and Colombia (around 40% in each).

Regarding the type of company where the respondents currently worked (see Fig. 1), most Argentinean respondents were employed in small companies, mainly those working in the office first mode. However, in the case of the remote mode group, the majority in all countries worked for large companies, with this percentage being notably higher among respondents from Spain (73%). In the case of the first office mode in Colombia, half was divided between local and national companies, while in Mexico 55% worked in multinational companies and in Spain, 47%. The companies where most people worked remotely were, therefore, generally multinational, and in office first mode they worked in local or national companies.

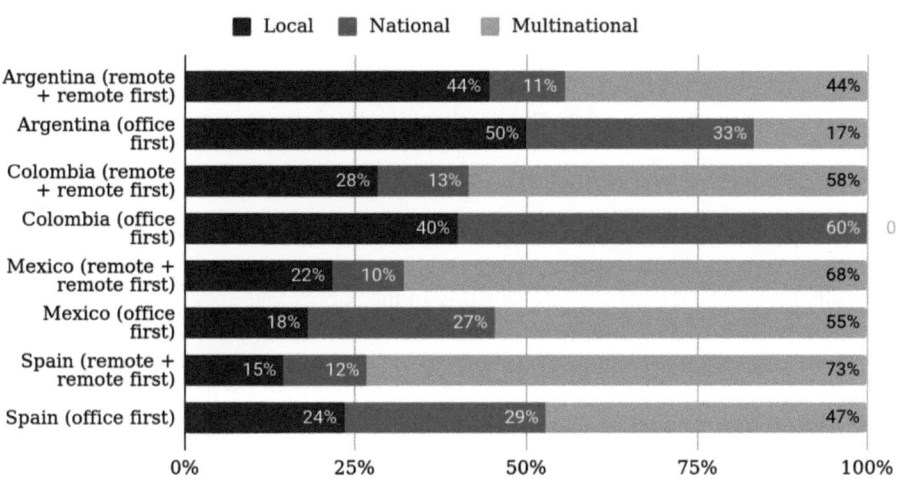

Fig. 1. Type of company where respondents work

In relation to work mode preferences, most respondents in all countries preferred remote or remote-first modes. Only in the case of those that worked in the office most days in Mexico (office first) did 55% preferred this mode. The same occurs in Spain with a 35%. Only a minority (less than 3% for all the countries) prefers the option of always working from the office (see Fig. 2). The respondents were also asked who chose the work modality they had. The results were the following. Argentina: decided by them, 8%; imposed by the company, 44%; consensual, 48%. Colombia: decided by them, 12.50%; imposed by the company, 43.75%; consensual, 43.75%. Mexico: decided by them, 11.88%; imposed by the company, 47.52%; consensual, 40.59%. Spain: decided by them, 18.64%; imposed by the company, 25.42%; consensual, 55.93%. Less than 50% of the cases were, in general, imposed by the company. In a nutshell, a significant portion of respondents in all countries reported that the decision was consensual between the company and themselves. Spain stands out with the highest percentage (18.64%) of respondents indicating that the decision was made by them. Finally, Mexico has the highest percentage (47.52%) of respondents stating that the work modality was imposed by the company.

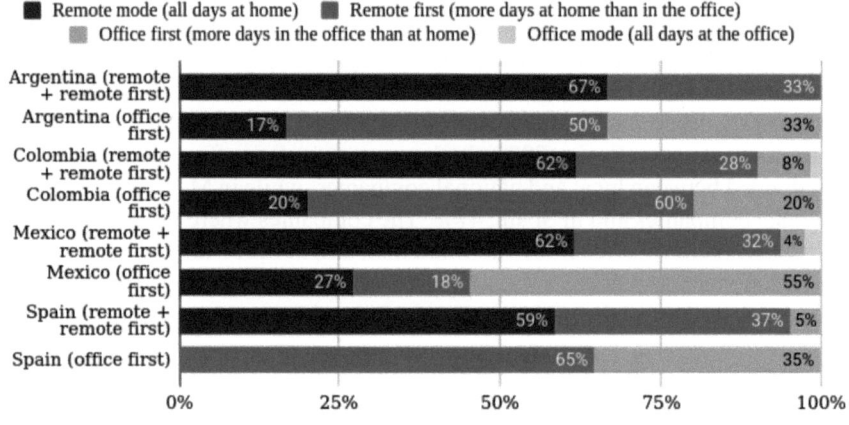

Fig. 2. Preferred work mode

4.2 Practitioners' Perception of Productivity

The following questions are related to the respondents' perceptions of their own work productivity under the current conditions, when compared to previous experiences of being fully present in the office. The wording in the survey was specifically: "I feel that my productivity is now…:", and the engineers had to choose one of the five options shown over Figs. 3 and 4. The data obtained indicates that in both cases (remote + remote first group and office first group), the respondents from all the countries reported higher productivity than when they went to the office every day. When we analysed the student's t-test for these two groups in relation to perceived productivity, we found a statistically significant difference (p-value = 0.005) between those who work mostly remotely (remote + remote first) and those who go to the office more frequently (office first).

We also evaluated whether there were significant differences between remote and office first workers by country. Spanish employees with high levels of remote work reported a higher performance (p = 0.027) compared with that of office first mode. Although the difference was not statistically significant for the other countries, Figs. 3 and 4 show descriptive trends. In the case of Argentina, almost 85% of office first group considered their productivity to be higher than when they went to the office every day. In the case of remote + remote first, it was around 45% for Argentineans, which is an important difference according to their work mode. Furthermore, more than 30% of them said that their productivity was "much higher than" when they went to the office every day. In Colombia and Mexico, respondents in the remote + remote first group also considered their productivity to be much higher. While in the office first, only and Mexico did some respondents consider their productivity to be much better than when they went to the office every day. The data seem, therefore, to indicate that the feeling of personal productivity is generally higher in the remote + remote first group than in the office first group, although both groups feel that their productivity is currently higher than before.

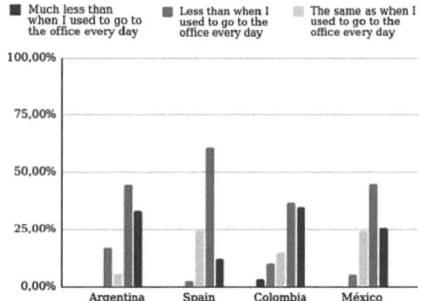

Fig. 3. Personal Productivity: Remote + remote first

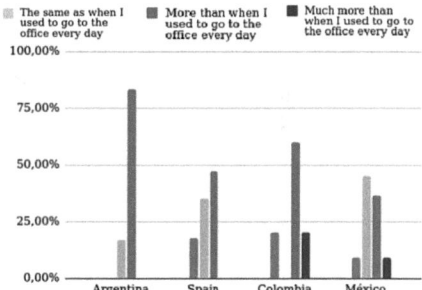

Fig. 4. Personal Productivity: Office first

We then asked about their perceptions about their team productivity, then the sentence was "I feel that the productivity of my team is…:". Figures 5 and 6 show the results obtained for this question. The t-test comparing the two groups (remote vs. office first mode) in terms of perceived team productivity did not reveal a statistically significant difference. However, the descriptive data highlighted some trends that may have implications deserving further examination.

In this case, the responses are different depending on the mode of work performed. In the case of remote + remote first (Fig. 5), in most countries the preferred response was "more than" and "much more than when I used to go to the office everyday ". Only in the case of Spain and Mexico was the second most-frequently chosen option: "The same as…". Moreover, only the number of responses from Colombia for the "The same as" option coincide with the number of responses for "Less than" option. In the case of office first (Fig. 6), only in Argentina they consider that their productivity was greater than when they went to the office every day. In the case of Colombia, 50% of those surveyed considered it to be "Less than" before. In general, therefore, the perception of the team's performance was that it was better than when they went to the office every day for the remote first group. In the case of office first, only one country (Argentina) considered that the productivity of their team was greater than when they went to the office every day. The remaining countries stated that the teams' productivity was the same or even less than when they went to the office every day.

As we wished to explore the perception of group work in greater depth, we formulated the following sentence: "I feel my team's capacity to meet milestones is:". The results are showed in Figs. 7 and 8, and they are quite similar to those obtained in the previous question. On the one hand, we did not find statistical significance when analysing the two groups in terms of their perception of milestone achievement. On the other hand, we believe it is worth discussing some patterns observed in the descriptive analysis. In the case of remote + remote first group (Fig. 7), the most frequently voted options were "more" and "the same than" except in the case of Argentina, where the number of people who indicated "much more" coincided with those who indicated that they did not have the information to answer the question. In the office first group (Fig. 8), the Colombian respondents again indicated that the ability to meet milestones was less that when they went to the office every day (50%) and the other half considered that it was "more or even much more", indicating that the Colombian office first had opposing opinions on this topic. The other countries oscillated between "The same" and "More than" options.

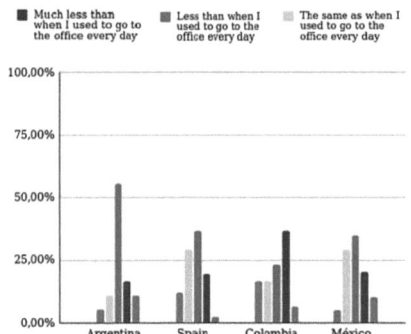

Fig. 5. Team Productivity - Remote + Remote First

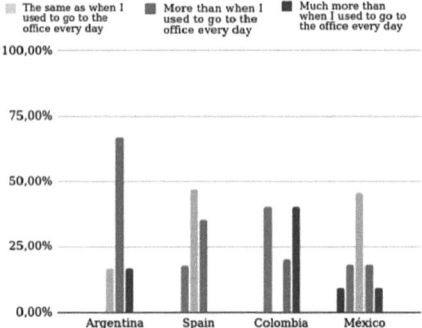

Fig. 6. Team Productivity - Office first

Overall, the data show that software practitioners have different perceptions according to their mode of work. In the case of remote or remote-first, the results regarding their own productivity, their team's productivity or their ability to meet milestones are quite or very optimistic. However, there is a wider range of opinions in the case of those who work most days in the office, including the opinion that the team's productivity is now worse, as is the case of Colombian professionals. However, 50% of respondents from Colombia also said they preferred remote mode while the other half were divided between the other types of work.

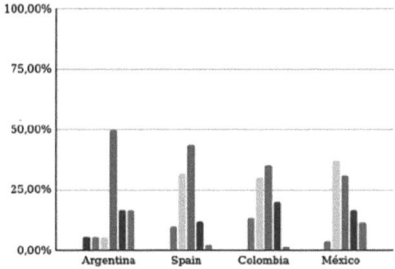
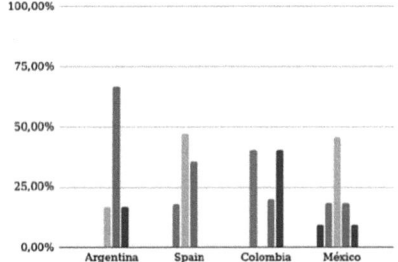

Fig. 7. My team's ability to meet milestones (Remote first)

Fig. 8. My team's ability to meet milestones (Office first)

4.3 Threats to Validity

The following are the threats to the validity of this work according to the dimensions identified by [12]. With regard to internal validity, fully controlling this threat is quite complicated when constructing a survey, since any error in a question can influence the respondent's answer. In our case, the same survey was to be used in all four countries, and this threat could consequently be even greater as the same word might not always have the same nuance in all four countries. The survey was, therefore, initially created by two researchers, one Spanish and one Colombian, who meticulously discussed each term to be used. Subsequently, the survey was reviewed by a senior psychologist (a former expert in stress and health at work) from Colombia), in order to check that the survey was well understood, unambiguous and did not guide the respondents' answers. It was then sent to the two Mexican authors who again refined it from the point of view of Mexican terminology, and it was reviewed by a statistics professor with experience in survey design. Finally, the same process took place in Argentina. An attempt was, therefore, made to diminish this threat to validity. With regard to external validity, a threat that prevents the generalisability of the results, we would like to clarify that since the respondents belong to four Spanish-speaking countries, the results obtained in this survey cannot be generalised to other countries. It would be interesting to carry it out in other countries of different cultures and compare the results. Another threat concerns the fact that most of the respondents preferred remote work and may have unconsciously stated that everything was better in this mode. However, in the survey, there were other questions, that have not been included in the paper owing to space constraints, to which the respondents indicated that the office mode was better, for example, such as the case of knowledge sharing. This fact could indicate that the respondents were sincere and answered what they really thought.

5 Conclusions

Employees' and employers' interests do not always coincide, there is currently a gap related to the convenience or otherwise of returning to the office to develop software. The results found in this study are quite interesting, as they indicate that most engineers prefer to work remotely (except in Colombia, where 50% of the sample had different opinions). When the engineers who mainly work remotely were asked about their perceptions of productivity, they generally indicated that it was the same or higher than when they worked in the office on a daily basis. If employers consider that a return to the office is opportune, they will, therefore, have to offer compensations, such as those suggested by [13], for instance, free parking, a more comfortable and calm work environment, or sport facilities.

Acknowledgments. Our thanks to Manuel Casas for his collaboration in the creation of the survey form and to Natalia Pinillas for her help in the creation of the graphs. Our thanks also go to all the engineers who answered the survey, without their collaboration this work would not have existed. Projects: OASSIS (PID2021-122554OB-C31), CALESI network (RED2022-134656-T), both funded by MCIN/ AEI /10. 13039/501100011033 / ERDF, EU, and by the EMMA project 'Evaluation and Improvement of the Environmental Sustainability of Applications', (SBPLY/21/180501/000115), financed by the Regional Ministry of Education, Culture and Sports of the Junta de Comunidades de Castilla La Mancha, and the European Regional Development Fund ERDF (Operational Programme of Castilla-La Mancha 2021–2027). Financial support for the implementation of applied research projects, within the framework of the UCLM Research Plan, 85% co-financed by the European Regional Development Fund (ERDF) UNION (2022-GRIN-34110).

References

1. Šmite, D., Christensen, E., Tell, P., Russo, D.: The future workplace: characterizing the spectrum of hybrid work arrangements for software teams. IEEE Softw. **40**(02), 34–41 (2023). https://doi.org/10.1109/ms.2022.3230289
2. Ebert, C., Vizcaíno, A., García, F., Suarez, J.: Measure and improve software. IEEE Softw. **41**(01), 35–44 (2024). https://doi.org/10.1109/MS.2023.3324466
3. Graziotin, D., Fagerholm, F.: Happiness and the productivity of software engineers. In: Sadowski, C., Zimmermann, T. (eds.) Rethinking Productivity in Software Engineering, pp. 109–124. Apress (2019)
4. Russo, D., Hanel, P., Altnickel, S., Van Berkel, N.: Predictors of well-being and productivity among software professionals during the COVID-19 pandemic – a longitudinal study. Empir. Softw. Eng. **26**(62) (2021). https://doi.org/10.1007/s10664-021-09945-9
5. Bezerra, C., et al: How human and organizational factors influence software teams' productivity in COVID-19 pandemic: a Brazilian survey. In: Proceedings of the 34th Brazilian Symposium on Software Engineering, pp. 606–615. ACM Digital Library. https://doi.org/10.1145/3422392.3422417 (2020)
6. Ahogado, A., Hoyos, J., Bocanegra, J., Gómez, V., Garcés, K.: Mining of repositories to understand productivity in remote work environments. In: Duque-Méndez, N., Aristizábábal-Quintero, L., Orozco-Alzate, M., Aguilar, J. (eds.) Advances in Computing. 18th Colombian Conference on Computing (CCC). Communications in Computer and Information Science, vol. 2209, pp. 407–421. Springer, Cham, Manizales, Colombia (2024). https://doi.org/10.1007/978-3-031-75236-0_29
7. Ahogado, A., Hoyos, J., Bocanegra, J., Góomez, V., Garcés, K.: Understanding productivity of colombian development teams working on remote environments. In Proceedings of the Ibero American Conference of Software Engineering (CIbSE), pp. 425–428 (2024b)

8. Ralph, P., et al.: Pandemic programming: How COVID-19 affects software developers and how their organizations can help. Empir. Softw. Eng. **25**(06), 4927–4961 (2020). https://doi.org/10.1007/s10664-020-09875-y
9. Ebert, C.: Industry Trends 2024: innovation needs competence. Computer **57**(4), 93–98 (2024). https://doi.org/10.1109/mc.2024.3364288
10. Vizcaíno, A., Suarez, J., Šmite, D., García, F.: Understanding remote work experience: insights into well-being. J. Softw.: Evol. Process **37**(1) (2025). https://doi.org/10.1002/smr.2757
11. Suárez, J., Vizcaíno, A.: Stress, motivation, and performance in global software engineering. J. Softw.: Evol. Process **36**(5) (2023). https://doi.org/10.1002/smr.2600
12. Wohlin, C., Runeson, P., Höst, M., Ohlsson, M., Regnell, B., Wesslén, A.: Experimentation in software engineering, vol. 236, pp. 123–151. Springer Berlin, Heidelberg (2012)
13. Šmite, D., Klotins, E., Moe, N.B.: What attracts employees to work on site in times of increased remote working?. IEEE Softw **42**(1), 100–109 (2025). https://doi.org/10.1109/MS.2024.337596

Open Access This chapter is licensed under the terms of the Creative Commons Attribution 4.0 International License (http://creativecommons.org/licenses/by/4.0/), which permits use, sharing, adaptation, distribution and reproduction in any medium or format, as long as you give appropriate credit to the original author(s) and the source, provide a link to the Creative Commons license and indicate if changes were made.

The images or other third party material in this chapter are included in the chapter's Creative Commons license, unless indicated otherwise in a credit line to the material. If material is not included in the chapter's Creative Commons license and your intended use is not permitted by statutory regulation or exceeds the permitted use, you will need to obtain permission directly from the copyright holder.

Understanding Factors Influencing Trust in Software Development Teams in Hybrid Work Settings: An Empirical Investigation

Sulabh Tyagi[1](✉) and Zainab Masood[2]

[1] Department of CSE & IT, Jaypee Institute of Information Technology, Noida, India
sulabhtyagi2k@yahoo.co.in
[2] Department of SE, CCIS, Prince Sultan University, Riyadh, Kingdom of Saudi Arabia

Abstract. The widespread adoption of hybrid work settings in software development has introduced new challenges in team collaboration, coordination, and trust-building. While hybrid work offers flexibility, it also reduces opportunities for informal interactions and shared identity formation, leading to communication gaps and trust deficits among team members. This study empirically examines the factors that influence trust in hybrid software development teams through 18 semi-structured interviews with practitioners from 10 software organizations in the USA, UK, and India. Using qualitative analysis, we identify five categories that represent multidimensional perspectives on trust in hybrid software development teams. Our findings emphasize the importance of these trust factors, providing software organizations with valuable insight to develop strategies to promote trust in hybrid teams.

Keywords: Trust · Hybrid · Software Development · Agile · Flexible

1 Introduction

The COVID-19 pandemic has accelerated the widespread adoption of hybrid work settings in software development teams worldwide. Hybrid work encompasses a variety of arrangements, including working from home, in-office work, remote work, and digital nomadism [19]. Griva et al. [7] defines hybrid work as *a socio-technical work arrangement, mediated by digital technology to enable collaboration among employees working at different times (e.g., synchronously and asynchronously) and in different locations (e.g., in the office and at home)*. Research confirms that the rapid transition to hybrid work in the software industry has introduced significant challenges, particularly in virtual collaboration and the building and maintaining trust within teams. A primary challenge in the hybrid work environment is the establishment of trust, as the opportunities for informal interactions are significantly reduced [11]. Temporal misalignments can lead to communication delays, further complicating the relationship building. In addition, remote teams often struggle to cultivate a shared identity and form strong interpersonal bonds due to the absence of in-person collaboration, even when videoconferencing tools are used [2]. Despite the widespread adoption of hybrid work settings, effective coordination and organization of tasks among employees across spatial and temporal boundaries remains a significant challenge. Smite et al. [16] highlight the need for strategic approaches to manage these complexities.

In a hybrid work setting, trust plays a crucial role in the creation of highperforming collaborative teams. Understanding how trust is established, sustained, and influenced in virtual work settings is vital for software development teams [12]. Caldwell et al. [1] reported that it is essential to examine the intricate dynamics of trust in hybrid teams and provide actionable strategies for organizations navigating this evolving work landscape. Advances in artificial intelligence (AI) and digital transformation are also shaping interpersonal and organizational trust, presenting challenges and opportunities to manage it in hybrid work settings [18]. Yet, there is still a lack of research on how trust is built and maintained in software development teams working in hybrid settings. Studying this is important for improving collaboration and team performance. Thus, we seek to answer the following research question: ***How is trust affected in software development teams in hybrid work settings?***

2 Background

Hybrid work has become a dominant arrangement in the post-pandemic software industry, blending on-site and remote work to provide employees with greater flexibility and autonomy [6].

Unlike distributed teams, which typically maintain a fixed remote structure, hybrid teams are more dynamic. Their configurations vary over time, with members alternating between working from the office and working remotely, or meeting face-to-face only occasionally [8].

As hybrid work becomes more common, it inherits many of the challenges traditionally associated with distributed teams, especially when it comes to building and maintaining trust. Trust has long been recognized as a critical enabler of collaboration in software development teams, particularly in distributed and remote contexts [17]. In such environments, limited informal interactions and a lack of shared context hinder the development of interpersonal trust. Existing research identifies challenges such as difficulties in evaluating the reliability of teammates, reduced visibility into work progress, and frequent misinterpretations due to asynchronous communication [5].

While hybrid teams share many of the trust-related challenges found in fully remote or distributed settings, they also introduce additional complexities. In hybrid environments, team members not only deal with physical and technical distance, but also with changing work patterns, such as sometimes working together in the office and other times working alone from different locations [8]. This variability can disrupt the development of shared norms, create asymmetries in access to information, and influence perceptions of fairness and inclusion, all of which directly impact trust dynamics [4]. Moreover, the reduced frequency of spontaneous in-person interactions can hinder team cohesion and limit the social bonds that are critical to trust and long-term team resilience.

These unique dynamics highlight the need to explore how trust is formed and sustained in hybrid teams. Although hybrid work is becoming increasingly common in software development, existing research has largely overlooked how trust works in these settings. Much of the current understanding stems from studies focused on either fully remote or fully co-located teams, which may not fully capture the complexities of hybrid environments. Given the distinct challenges and work patterns in hybrid teams, it is essential to explore the factors that influence trust and how it is built and maintained within this context. This study addresses this gap by examining the socio-technical conditions that shape trust in hybrid software development teams.

Table 1. Participants' Demographics

Participant #	Role	Country	Development Method	Team Size	Office Days
P1, P3	Tester & Team Leader	India	Waterfall	30	3
P2, P18	Developer & Business Analyst	UK	Scrum	15	1–2
P4	UX Designer	UK	Waterfall	23	3
P5, P7	Agile Coach, Product Owner	USA	Scrum & XP	18	2
P6, P17	Product Owner (PO) & Director-Delivery	India	Scrum & XP	25	4
P8	Product Owner	UK	Scrum	12	3
P9	Senior Project Manager	India	Waterfall	34	3–4
P10, P11	Scrum Master & Product Manager	USA	Scrum & Kanban	17	3
P12, P13	QA Engineer & Test Manager	India	Waterfall	23	2–3
P14, P15, P16	Scrum Master (SM), Technical Architect, Chief Story Teller	USA	Scrum & XP	18	3

3 Research Method

Our objective was to explore the perspectives of practitioners on various factors that influence software development teams in hybrid work environments. We collected data through interviews with 18 software practitioners from ten IT companies in the USA, UK, and India (demographics represented in Table 1) over 10 months (3 February to 9 November 2024). We used purposive sampling to recruit participants who were currently working in a hybrid work environment. The sample included practitioners in various roles such as Agile coaches, project managers, delivery managers, testers, developers, product owners, Scrum

Table 2. Data Analysis Process showing Emergence of Category Leadership from underlying Concepts

Participants' Quotes	Codes	Concepts
"You need to be approachable... it's the first thing ...to build trust in your team in this [Hybrid Set up]. Every team member should have access to you, whether they work remotely or in the office." **P5, Agile Coach**	Approachable Leadership for Trust-Building, Leader Accessibility, Building Trust	Trust through Approachable Leadership
"So, there was a manager...to approach him was difficult, I missed that leadership support. I think that readiness and ease to contact your leader at any time, particularly in a hybrid work environment, is crucial in building trust." **P1, Tester**	Supportive Leadership for Trust, Open Communication, Building Trust	Trust through Accessible Leadership
"A leader should not make project decisions solely with the team members present in the office. Leadership should be fair to everyone. They should involve remote team members as well in important decisions to create an environment of trust." **P3, Team Leader**	Inclusive Decision-Making, Fair Leadership, Trust-Centered Leadership	Trust through Inclusive & Fair Leadership

masters, and technical architects, all with 3 to 20 years of experience in IT development and at least one year in a hybrid setting (as shown in Table 1). To ensure diversity, we selected participants from a variety of industry domains, including telecom, digital, EdTech, healthcare, e-commerce, insurance, and banking & finance. This allowed us to explore hybrid work practices in different organizational contexts. The size of the participating software organizations ranged from 500 to 400,000 employees.

To facilitate in-depth discussions, we developed an open-ended semi-structured interview guide that allowed participants to share their perspectives on the most critical aspects. Before data collection, we evaluated the relevance and effectiveness of the guide by seeking feedback from six leading professionals and academics in the field. Based on their feedback, we incorporated the suggestions for improvements into the final version of the guide.

To maintain ethical concerns, we kept the identities of the participants confidential. With their consent, we audio-recorded all interviews and transcribed them upon completion for further analysis. We conducted data collection and analysis simultaneously. A total of ten interviews were conducted online using Microsoft Teams. For all interviews (online and in person), the duration ranged from 35 to 60 min During interviews, participants were asked about their experiences in hybrid work environments, the differences between working in the office and at home, the challenges associated with each setting, and the impact of hybrid work on coordination and trust. Some sample questions from the guide are: *Q: How would you define trust and its importance in hybrid work settings? Q: What factors do you believe contribute to building or eroding trust in your hybrid team? Q: How does leadership behavior impact trust in the hybrid software team? Q: What role does your organization play in this hybrid work culture? How does it influence trust? Q: How do you collaborate and manage work with remote or in-office team members?*

We employed open coding and constant comparison methods for qualitative data analysis [14]. We divided the interview transcripts into discrete segments, followed by open coding to identify incidents that illustrated key aspects of trust dynamics in hybrid software development teams. We then grouped the key incidents from each segment and assigned them a representative code to summarize the key point. Through constant comparison, we analyzed codes from one interview alongside those from other interviews, allowing us to group similar codes into broader concepts that represent the second level of abstraction. We then repeat this process on concepts to derive higher-level categories. Table 2 provides an overview of the data analysis process applied in this study.

4 Results

This section outlines the factors influencing trust in hybrid work settings. Relevant interview excerpts are integrated into the descriptions of each category for a better understanding.

4.1 Leadership

Leadership factors encompass qualities that influence trust in a hybrid work environment. Most of the participants reported that leadership plays a pivotal role in building and maintaining trust in hybrid teams, as employees are not always physically present together. It is the leader's responsibility to ensure equal access to information and opportunities for both in-office and remote employees. The supporting quotes are provided in Table 2, highlighting the role of leadership in fostering trust through *Approachable, Accessible,* and *Inclusive & Fair* leadership.

When remote workers feel isolated, it can result in a lack of trust within the team, as they find fewer opportunities to engage with colleagues and leaders. The absence of informal interactions or timely support can hinder the development of relationships and mutual understanding. P5 emphasized the importance of accessibility to the leader in this context:

"You need to be approachable..., it's the first thing you must do to build trust in your team in this [hybrid setup]. Every team member should have access to you, whether they work remotely or in the office." P5, Agile Coach

Including every team member in important project decisions is essential to foster trust. A majority of participants emphasized that leaders must involve

both in-office and remote employees in key decision-making processes; otherwise, remote workers may feel excluded, which can weaken trust.
"I must tell you ..in a hybrid environment, a leader's role becomes even more critical since not all team members are in the office on the same days. This means adopting a people-first approach to addressing concerns, rather than resorting to micromanagement, which can erode trust." P14, SM

4.2 Organizational

We found that trust in hybrid teams is also influenced by organizational factors such as hybrid work policies, performance appraisal processes, and workplace facilities.

Many participants highlighted the need to provide flexibility to employees in hybrid settings to foster trust.
"Organizations... adapting to a hybrid workplace while building a high-trust team is not an additional effort they need to provide flexible work policies that cater to every employee." - P17, Director-Delivery
"Organizational culture, including how hybrid work policies are designed and the level of... crucial role in establishing trust." - P15, Technical Architect

Another critical aspect of organizational culture that directly impacts trust is the performance appraisal system. A fair and transparent evaluation process is essential to foster trust in hybrid teams. When assessment criteria are unclear or biased toward in-office employees, remote workers can feel undervalued and disengaged, leading to a breakdown of trust and being demotivated.

Senior managers emphasized that lack of transparency in appraisal systems could hinder trust building in hybrid teams, underscoring the importance of clear KPIs and fair evaluation criteria for remote and in-office employees, as quoted by P9.
"If your organization does not have a transparent appraisal system that evaluates both remote and in-office employees equally, it may create challenges in building trust..." - P9, Sr. Project Manager

4.3 Personal Attributes

In hybrid work settings, the personality traits of the team members play a crucial role in fostering a healthy team environment. Team members who are open to sharing knowledge, eager to learn new things, and demonstrate empathy are reported to contribute significantly to building trust.
"One crucial factor... is your personality. It's about how willingly you help others, your eagerness to learn new things, and how quickly you share project information with your team. These behaviors foster trust." - P6, PO

In a hybrid work environment, a *self-first attitude* can undermine trust. If team members focus only on their own achievements rather than contributing to the team as a whole, trust can break down. Hybrid teams function best when everyone works collectively rather than prioritizing themselves individually.

"Are you only concerned about yourself in every discussion? Do you only focus on your growth in every task? it's 'we,' not 'I,' that matters in a hybrid team. A self-first attitude can negatively impact trust within the team." P16, Chief Story Teller

4.4 Digital Technology

Many practitioners reported that digital tools serve as the backbone of communication, collaboration, and task management in hybrid work settings. However, when these tools are poorly integrated or difficult to use, they can disrupt teamwork and create frustration, ultimately affecting trust among team members.

"We encountered an issue with a poorly integrated tool–while using Asana, task updates in Asana did not reflect consistently across projects. This hindered collaboration and ultimately impacted trust across teams." - P13, Test Manager

While AI-powered tools offer opportunities for efficiency and automation in performing tasks, their use for employee monitoring, such as productivity tracking and keystroke logging, can create an atmosphere of distrust. Employees may perceive such surveillance measures as a lack of confidence in their work, leading to disengagement and reduced morale. Striking a balance between leveraging technology for productivity and building employee trust is essential for a healthy hybrid work environment. As one participant noted,

"...adopting new digital technologies and tools [in hybrid], but at the same time, AI tools such as productivity tracking and keystroke monitoring create low trust among employees making them feel like they are not trusted." - P10, SM.

Another participant reflected on the broader post-pandemic shift as:

"Post-COVID era has introduced many new things, with hybrid working being one, particularly in IT... recent advancements in AI provide employers with multiple options, including employee surveillance and monitoring. This must be balanced to ensure it does not undermine employee trust." -P5, Agile Coach.

4.5 Communication

Communication plays a crucial role in both building and breaking trust within hybrid software development teams. Our findings indicate that different attributes of communication, i.e., *lack of communication, transparent communication, informal communication,* and *outside work communication* influence trust.

Differing hybrid work schedules can cause communication gaps, leading to misunderstandings and reduced trust, as managers note below.

".. That's when trust comes into play so if our [in-office and remote] teams working in different time zones do not exhibit good communication then it will affect trust and ultimately our time critical decisions". - P10, Scrum Master

".. some team members do not communicate their concerns [to me or to other members] and I think that communication gap hinders trust." - P6, PO

Therefore, open and transparent communication is essential to build trust, especially in key decision-making meetings when done online, such as monthly

releases, sprint planning, and backlog refinement sessions. Poor communication in these meetings can negatively impact both trust and critical decisions.
"more than half of us perform our meetings and work online and transparent communication is incredibly important for building trust." - P4, UX Designer

Participants noted that trust in hybrid teams extends beyond work, requiring personal connections. With varying schedules and time zones, managers and team members must actively foster trust through informal interactions like virtual coffee chats and team-building activities.
"Trust... only business talks, You need to indulge in some fun activity, virtual coffee chats or... to boost that [trust] up" - P18, Business Analyst

5 Discussion and Conclusion

This study highlights key factors that influence trust in hybrid teams. Findings reveal that the absence of spontaneous and informal interactions in hybrid teams often hinders the development of interpersonal trust. Fair and inclusive leadership emerged as a critical component in fostering trust, as also supported by other studies [9]. Effective inclusive leadership not only enhances collaboration and performance, but also strengthens trust in hybrid teams by balancing the needs of remote and in-office employees while ensuring that all members feel valued and included [9]. Shared decision-making and organizational policies are key to fostering workplace trust. Transparent performance appraisals and equitable treatment of remote and in-office employees strengthen trust, especially in hybrid teams. These findings support the idea that clear work policies allow team members to choose flexible work arrangements that best suit their needs [15].

While digital technology improves collaboration in hybrid teams, our findings reveal its positive and negative effects on trust building. A key concern among the participants was the AI-powered employee monitoring tools, such as productivity tracking and keystroke recording. Although designed to improve efficiency, these tools can create a sense of surveillance, ultimately undermining employee trust. This highlights the need for algorithmic management to balance productivity with employee autonomy to sustain trust in hybrid work environments [10].

Our findings also emphasize the integral role of team communication in shaping trust dynamics. Transparent and consistent communication fosters trust, but time zone mismatches can create communication barriers and weaken it. One study identified communication breakdowns and the resulting distrust as key risk factors that undermine coordination in hybrid teams [3]. We also found that personality attributes significantly impact trust in hybrid teams. A self-centered attitude weakens trust, while collaboration and empathy foster a supportive environment, as reported in [13], highlighting the need for further exploration.

This study contributes to the growing literature on trust in hybrid work environments by providing empirical evidence on key factors influencing trust dynamics. Our insights can help organizations design policies and leadership strategies that foster trust, ultimately enhancing team collaboration and performance. For future work, we intend to develop actionable strategies for building and sustaining trust in hybrid teams, with direct implications for the Software Engineering community. These insights will help enhance collaboration, leadership, and team dynamics in distributed work environments. We also plan to expand this study by developing a comprehensive framework for fostering sustainable trust in hybrid work environments utilising both qualitative and quantitative methods.

Acknowledgement. We sincerely thank the practitioners for their time and for sharing their valuable experiences. This research study is partially supported by the PDF grant from JIIT, India. We also thank Prince Sultan University for their support in this research.

References

1. Caldwell, S., et al.: A research framework for hybrid human-AI teaming: trust, transparency, and transferability. ACM Trans. Interact. Intell. Syst. **12**(3), 1–36 (2022)
2. Conboy, K., et al.: Temporal complexity and business value in analytics. Inf. Manag. **57**(1), 103077 (2020)
3. de Souza Santos, R., et al.: A grounded theory of coordination in remote-first and hybrid teams. In Proceedings of 44th International Conference on Software Engineering, pp. 25–35 (2022)
4. de Souza Santos, R., Adisaputri, G., Ralph, P.: Post-pandemic resilience of hybrid software teams. In: 2023 IEEE/ACM 16th International Conference on Cooperative and Human Aspects of Software Engineering (CHASE), pp. 1–12. IEEE (2023)
5. Fiol, C.M., O'Connor, E.J.: Identification in face-to-face, hybrid, and pure virtual teams: Untangling the contradictions. Organization science (2005)
6. Gibson, C.B., et al.: Should employees be required to return to the office? Organ. Dyn. **52**(2), 100981 (2023)
7. Griva, A., et al.: Making space for time: Strategies for designing time-aware hybrid work. Syst. J. Inf. (2024)
8. Handke, L., et al.: Hybrid teamwork: what we know and where we can go from here. Small Group Res. **55**(5), 805–835 (2024)
9. Hincapie, M.X., Costa, P.: Fostering hybrid team performance through inclusive leadership. Organ. Dyn. **53**(3), 101072 (2024)
10. Jeffrey, A., Thorpe, H.: Relational ethics in pandemic research: vulnerabilities and becoming together-apart. Qual. Inq. **30**(1), 101–113 (2024)
11. Larsson, J., Revland, S.: Trust and knowledge sharing in hybrid project teams (2023)
12. Mancl, D., Fraser, S.D.: The future of work: Agile in a hybrid world. In: International Conference on Agile Software Development, pp. 63–70. Springer (2022)
13. Paasivaara, M., Wang, X.: The spectrum of hybrid work in software engineering: research directions. In: International Conference on Agile Software Development, pp. 139–148. Springer (2022)
14. Seaman, C.B.: Qualitative methods in software engineering research. IEEE Trans. Softw. Eng. **25**(4), 557–572 (1999)
15. Smite, D., et al.: The future workplace: hybrid work arrangements in software teams. IEEE Softw. **40**(2), 34–41 (2022)

16. Smite, D., et al.: From forced WFH to voluntary working-from-anywhere: Two revolutions in telework. J. Syst. Softw. **195**, 111509 (2023)
17. Tyagi, S., et al.: Empirically developed framework for building trust in distributed agile teams. Inf. Softw. Technol. **145**, 106828 (2022)
18. Veselov, Y.V.: Trust in a digital society (2020)
19. Wang, B., et al.: Beyond the factory paradigm: digital nomadism and the digital future (s) of knowledge work post-COVID-19. J. Assoc. Inf. Syst. **21**(6), 10 (2020)

Open Access This chapter is licensed under the terms of the Creative Commons Attribution 4.0 International License (http://creativecommons.org/licenses/by/4.0/), which permits use, sharing, adaptation, distribution and reproduction in any medium or format, as long as you give appropriate credit to the original author(s) and the source, provide a link to the Creative Commons license and indicate if changes were made.

The images or other third party material in this chapter are included in the chapter's Creative Commons license, unless indicated otherwise in a credit line to the material. If material is not included in the chapter's Creative Commons license and your intended use is not permitted by statutory regulation or exceeds the permitted use, you will need to obtain permission directly from the copyright holder.

Towards a closer collaboration between practice and research in Agile Software Development – What we learnt; and what not?

Towards a Closer Collaboration Between Practice and Research in Agile Software Development Workshop: A Summary and Research Agenda

Michael Neumann[1](✉)[iD], Eva-Maria Schön[2][iD], Mali Senapathi[3][iD], Maria Rauschenberger[2][iD], and Tiago Silva da Silva[4][iD]

[1] University of Applied Sciences Hannover, Hannover, Germany
michael.neumann@hs-hannover.de
[2] University of Applied Sciences Emden/Leer, Emden/Leer, Germany
{eva-maria.schon,maria.rauschenberger}@hs-emden-leer.de
[3] Auckland University of Technology, Auckland, New Zealand
mali.senapathi@aut.ac.nz
[4] Federal University of São Paulo, São Paulo, Brazil
silva.tiago@unifesp.br

Abstract. Agile software development principles and values have been widely adopted across various industries, influencing products and services globally. Despite its increasing popularity, a significant gap remains between research and practical implementation. This paper presents the findings of the first international workshop designed to foster collaboration between research and practice in agile software development. We discuss the main themes and factors identified by the workshop participants that contribute to this gap, strategies to bridge it, and the challenges that require further research attention.

Keywords: Agile Methods · theory · practice · collaboration · workshop

1 Introduction

Agile software development has gained high interest in research and practice for more than 20 years. Many phenomena have been examined in detail, and a considerable body of knowledge has been created. Examples of this include today's detailed understanding of human-centered software development [10,14,19,21], agile requirements [18], the scaling of agile approaches [5,6], measuring agility [11] and the well-known challenges posed by remote/distributed work [13]. However, a significant gap persists between the research on agile software development and practice. The key factors that have led to this gap include the evolving, complex, and multifaceted nature of practitioner problems, the perception of research as irrelevant to practice, the complexity of organizational contexts, and the difficulty in addressing systemic issues [1]. A study highlights the importance of fostering collaboration and joint research efforts between academia and practice to bridge the gap between academic research and industry practices in managing requirements in agile software development [4]. This collaboration can help raise awareness and address challenges and opportunities at the intersection of requirements and agile software development [4,8,23]. Other examples include integrating user experience (UX) into agile projects [19], DevOps in agile [20], large-scale agile, dependency management in agile projects, and applying agile values and practices in higher education [17].

To ensure that academic research addresses specific practitioner needs effectively, we identified two highly relevant gaps to start with:

1. The *theory-gap* in agile research: Research within the agile community mainly consists of empirical case studies, typical in an interdisciplinary field like agile software development. However, practitioners express concerns about the external validity of case studies and question whether the findings can be generalized to the broader industry [22]. Furthermore, many academic contributions reveal other aspects of the theory gap. A recent review of large-scale agile methods highlights several theoretical and practical issues in the existing literature, such as an overemphasis on the practices of agile frameworks at the expense of the foundational theoretical principles outlined in the Agile Manifesto [2]. For instance, while large-scale agile transformations have been widely studied, there is a noticeable lack of theoretical developments on managing and sustaining their implementation [3]. Therefore, academic research is vital to develop theories that can enhance agile practices and processes and improve software outcomes, and thus provide a solid foundation for future empirical research [16,22].
2. The *time-gap* between practice and research: For two decades, agile practice has outpaced research. The adaptation of continuous improvement processes has resulted in a wide variety of agile practices in the industry. Furthermore, since 2020, we have been experiencing an era of rapidly accelerating disruptive changes, such as the transition to remote work and the integration of Artificial Intelligence (AI) technologies into existing software development processes. In practice, while agile teams, particularly those with high maturity, demonstrate resilience in adapting to address these challenges, research is struggling to keep up and, metaphorically speaking, to get into the *"driver's seat"* to actively shape these emerging trends. It is essential to balance the different timescales between research and industrial problems to produce research outcomes that are relevant and valuable to the industry [24].

This paper summarizes the half-day workshop held at the International Conference on Agile Software Development, XP 2025 (XP2025). The workshop aimed to establish a foundation for fostering closer collaboration between researchers and practitioners, ensuring that academic research better addresses the needs of practitioners. It provided an interactive platform for sharing knowledge and exchanging experiences between academics and industry professionals.

2 Workshop Results

This section presents the results of our workshop, held on Monday, 2nd June 2025, as part of the XP2025 conference. It consisted of three parts: (1) The first part was dedicated to setting the stage, clarifying the workshop's objectives, and ensuring a shared understanding among participants by introducing and explaining the definitions of the theory-gap and time-gap. (2) This was followed by a moderated panel discussion featuring four invited panelists, which lasted approximately 60 min. Participants were encouraged to contribute actively by asking questions and making comments. (3) The third part consisted of a *World Café* session (approximately 60 min), during which participants engaged in group discussions on the identified gaps. The workshop ended with collaborative data synthesis. Further material on the workshop, such as slides and photos of the results, are available in a repository [15].

2.1 Panel Discussion

In this part of the workshop, a panel with 4 panelists was held. The panelists included: Karen Eilers, Owner of the Institute of Information in Hamburg and a Lecturer at both the University of St. Gallen in Switzerland and Offenburg University of Applied Sciences; Nan Yang, Co-founder and Product Owner at Man Yi Education Consulting from 2017 to 2021, currently pursuing a PhD on ambidextrous software startups at LUT University in Lahti, Finland; Marcelo Luis Walter, Consulting Business Unit Manager at Objective Solutions in Brazil and a PhD candidate in Artificial Intelligence at the Pontifical Catholic University of Paraná in Curitiba, Brazil; and Tiago Silva da Silva, a Professor at the Federal University of São Paulo, Brazil.

2.2 World Café session

In the World Café, workshop participants ($N = 6$) expanded on their arguments through discussion and clustered them on brown paper using sticky notes. Photos of the activity are available in a repository [15]. The key points are summarized below.

*The following key points regarding the **theory-gap** were discussed:*

- Standardization of keywords.
- Abstracts without *"Click-bating description"*.
- Promote oral formats, such as videos, podcasts, and blog posts; researchers should also be evaluated based on these.
- Develop new KPIs beyond traditional papers' metrics; introduce alternative metrics for research evaluation (*e.g.,* productivity) while addressing challenges in measuring different outcomes.
- Cross-disciplinary studies, action research, and longitudinal studies.
- Increase accessibility through more open-access research, but address the funding question: Who will cover the costs?

- Abstraction *vs.* speed/return on investment.
- Researchers and practitioners working together on one project (risk of bias).
- Researchers should speak at practitioners' conferences and use simpler language.

*The following key points regarding the **time-gap** were discussed:*

- Split projects into more little pieces; overlapping phases.
- Maybe not always aim on closing the time-gap? *"We need some time to make it right"*.
- Rapid release reporting, write papers and publish preprints; publish first, present later; medicine as a role model; this requires cultural shift.
- Propose small-scale experiments (MVPs).
- Grant models vs. incremental deliverables.
- Is the context chaotic or complex?

3 Agenda for Future Research

The industry's primary focus remains on delivering impactful results and ensuring a strong return on investment [22]. The workshop participants underscored the pivotal role that academia plays in validating the inherent unpredictability of the industry, where outcomes often stem from ill-informed decision-making, and reproducibility remains challenging due to a lack of clarity about how these results were achieved. This is where the contribution of academic research becomes vital: it seeks to clarify, through the scientific method, how successful strategies in one context can be adapted and applied to seemingly unrelated situations. As a result, any contributions from academic research that improve outcomes, reduce costs, improve efficiency, or facilitate the measurement of productivity are likely to attract significant interest [22].

Several recommendations were proposed during the workshop to bridge the gaps between researchers and practitioners, particularly concerning theory and time. To address the theory-gap, suggestions included having researchers create diverse media formats – such as videos, podcasts, and blog posts – and using research methods, like Design Science Research and action research, that directly address industry challenges. Additionally, making academic research more accessible through open access and presenting findings in simpler language for industry practitioners were highlighted as important steps.

To mitigate the *time-gap*, rapid dissemination of academic publications was suggested, including white papers and preprints. Central to addressing these gaps is the imperative to foster strong collaboration and meaningful relationships between researchers and practitioners. The challenges associated with *time-* and theory-gap are apparent in *Mode 1* research, which adheres to scientific principles but produces outcomes that are primarily relevant to the academic community, offering limited value to businesses [9]. In contrast, *Mode 2* research [12] adopts a collaborative model that bridges academic rigour with practical applicability by involving multi-stakeholder teams, comprising both academics and practitioners, who work together to address real-world problems [7]. *Mode 2* is built on several key principles: solving problems within specific application contexts, engaging in cross-disciplinary problem-solving that integrates theoretical and empirical elements, ensuring social accountability for research outcomes while cultivating a deeper understanding of diverse perspectives, and implementing quality controls that extend beyond traditional academic peer review to encompass the practical implications and impact of research [1]. This suggests that researchers must adopt a *Mode 2* collaborative research model to address some of the challenges related to time and theory gaps. Nevertheless, *Mode 2* comes (as every research model) with limitations. While applying *Mode 2* the generalizability of the results can be one of the major threats to validity. Although the workshop did not provide absolute predictions regarding future research problems or questions, the discussions indicated that numerous inquiries related to contemporary topics – such as the integration of AI and DevOps in agile development and large-scale agile transformations – could be explored using a *Mode 2* collaborative approach to address the theoretical and temporal gaps discussed during the workshop.

4 Conclusion

To address the challenges related to the *theory-* and *time- gap* between research and practice in agile software development, we organized the first international workshop at the XP2025 conference. This workshop provided an interactive platform for panelists and participants to critically reflect on and discuss the key issues in bridging the divide between researchers and practitioners in agile software development. Our aim was to identify the main themes related to theory and time gaps, foster a community of researchers interested in this subject, and develop an agenda for future research. We plan to continue building a community of researchers and practitioners, addressing the theory and time gaps through future workshops, and identifying specific industry-relevant research topics and questions that academia can explore.

References

1. Barroca, L., Sharp, H., Salah, D., Taylor, K., Gregory, P.: Bridging the gap between research and agile practice: an evolutionary model. Int. J. Syst. Assur. Eng. Manag. **9**(2), 323–334 (2015). https://doi.org/10.1007/s13198-015-0355-5
2. Beck, K., et al.: Agile manifesto (2021). https://agilemanifesto.org/
3. Carroll, N., Conboy, K., Wang, X.: From transformation to normalisation: an exploratory study of a large-scale agile transformation. J. Inf. Technol. **38**(3), 267–303 (2023). https://doi.org/10.1177/02683962231164428
4. Barroca, L., Sharp, H., Salah, D., Taylor, K., Gregory, P.: Bridging the gap between research and agile practice: an evolutionary model. Int. J. Syst. Assur. Eng. Manag. **9**(2), 323–334 (2015). https://doi.org/10.1007/s13198-015-0355-5

5. Dingsoeyr, T., Falessi, D., Power, K.: Agile development at scale: the next frontier. IEEE Softw. **36**(2), 30–38 (2019). https://doi.org/10.1109/MS.2018.2884884
6. Dingsøyr, T., Moe, N.B., Fægri, T.E., Seim, E.A.: Exploring software development at the very large-scale: a revelatory case study and research agenda for agile method adaptation. Empir. Softw. Eng. **23**(1), 490–520 (2017). https://doi.org/10.1007/s10664-017-9524-2
7. Gray, D., Iles, P., Watson, S.: Spanning the HRD academic-practitioner divide: bridging the gap through mode 2 research. J. Eur. Ind. Train. **35**, 247–263 (2011)
8. Gregory, P., Barroca, L., Sharp, H., Deshpande, A., Taylor, K.: The challenges that challenge: engaging with agile practitioners' concerns. Inf. Softw. Technol. **77**, 92–104 (2016). https://doi.org/10.1016/j.infsof.2016.04.006
9. Huff, A., Huff, J.: Re-focusing the business school agenda. Br. J. Manag. **12**, S49–S54 (2001)
10. Kuchel, T., Neumann, M., Diebold, P., Schön, E.M.: Which challenges do exist with agile culture in practice? In: Proceedings of the Symposium on Applied Computing, pp. 1018–1025 (2023). https://doi.org/10.1145/3555776.3578726
11. Looks, H., Fangmann, J., Thomaschewski, J., Escalona, M., Schön, E.M.: Towards a standardized questionnaire for measuring agility at team level. In: Agile Processes in Software Engineering and Extreme Programming. XP 2021, pp. 71–85 (2021)
12. MacLean, D., MacIntosh, R., Grant, S.: Mode 2 management research. Br. J. Manag. **13**, 189–207 (2002)
13. Neumann, M., Bogdanov, Y.: The impact of COVID 19 on agile software development: a systematic literature review. In: Proceedings of the 55th Hawaii International Conference on System Sciences (2022). https://doi.org/10.24251/HICSS.2022.882
14. Neumann, M., Kuchel, T., Diebold, P., Schön, E.M.: Agile culture clash: unveiling challenges in cultivating an agile mindset in organizations. Comput. Sci. Inf. Syst. **21**(3), 1013–1031 (2024). https://doi.org/10.2298/CSIS230715029N
15. Neumann, N., Schöon, E.M., Senapathi, M., Rauschenberger, M., da Silva, T.S.: Additional material to workshop agilepr at xp2025 (2025). bit.ly/xp2025-agilepr1
16. Schmid, K.: If you want better empirical research, value your theory: on the importance of strong theories for progress in empirical software engineering research. In: Proceedings of the 25th International Conference on Evaluation and Assessment in Software Engineering, pp. 359–364. Association for Computing Machinery, New York, NY, USA (2021). https://doi.org/10.1145/3463274.3463360
17. Schön, E.M., Buchem, I., Sostak, S., Rauschenberger, M.: Shift toward value-based learning: applying agile approaches in higher education. In: Marchiori, M., Domínguez Mayo, F.J., Filipe, J. (eds.) Web Information Systems and Technologies, pp. 24–41. Springer Nature Switzerland, Cham (2023)
18. Schön, E., Winter, D., Escalona, M., Thomaschewski, J.: Key challenges in agile requirements engineering. In: Proceedings of the18th International Conference on Agile Software Development. Springer, Cham (2017)
19. Schön, E.M., Silva da Silva, T., Hinderks, A., Sharp, H., Thomaschewski, J.: Introduction to special issue on agile UX: challenges, successes and barriers to improvement. Inf. Softw. Technol. **158**, 107193 (2023)
20. Senapathi, M., Buchan, J., Osman, H.: DevOps capabilities, practices, and challenges: insights from a case study. In: Proceedings of the 22nd International Conference on Evaluation and Assessment in Software Engineering 2018, pp. 57–67. EASE '18, Association for Computing Machinery, New York, NY, USA (2018). https://doi.org/10.1145/3210459.3210465

21. Šmite, D., Gonzalez-Huerta, J., Moe, N.B.: "when in Rome, do as the romans do": cultural barriers to being agile in distributed teams. In: Proceedings of the International Conference on Agile Software Development, pp. 145–161 (2020)
22. Winters, T.: Thoughts on applicability. J. Syst. Softw. **215**, 112086 (2024). https://doi.org/10.1016/j.jss.2024.112086
23. Wohlin, C., et al.: The success factors powering industry-academia collaboration. IEEE Softw. **29**(2), 67–73 (2012). https://doi.org/10.1109/MS.2011.92
24. Woods, E.: Dear researchers step 1: find a team with a problem. J. Syst. Softw. **222**, 112318 (2025)

Open Access This chapter is licensed under the terms of the Creative Commons Attribution 4.0 International License (http://creativecommons.org/licenses/by/4.0/), which permits use, sharing, adaptation, distribution and reproduction in any medium or format, as long as you give appropriate credit to the original author(s) and the source, provide a link to the Creative Commons license and indicate if changes were made.

The images or other third party material in this chapter are included in the chapter's Creative Commons license, unless indicated otherwise in a credit line to the material. If material is not included in the chapter's Creative Commons license and your intended use is not permitted by statutory regulation or exceeds the permitted use, you will need to obtain permission directly from the copyright holder.

Posters Track

Lessons from a Big-Bang Integration: Challenges in Edge Computing and Machine Learning

Alessandro Aneggi(✉) and Andrea Janes

Free University of Bozen-Bolzano, Bolzano, Italy
{aaneggi,ajanes}@unibz.it

Abstract. This experience report analyses a one-year project focused on building a distributed real-time analytics system using edge computing and machine learning. The project faced critical setbacks due to a "big-bang" integration approach, where all components–developed by multiple geographically dispersed partners–were merged at the final stage. The integration effort resulted in only six minutes of system functionality, far below the expected 40 min. Through root cause analysis, the study identifies technical and organisational barriers, including poor communication, lack of early integration testing, and resistance to top-down planning. It also considers psychological factors such as a bias toward fully developed components over mock-ups. The paper advocates for early mock-based deployment, robust communication infrastructures, and the adoption of top-down thinking to manage complexity and reduce risk in reactive, distributed projects. These findings underscore the limitations of traditional Agile methods in such contexts and propose simulation-driven engineering and structured integration cycles as key enablers for future success.

Keywords: big-bang integration · reactive applications · retrospective

1 Introduction

This report reflects on last year's project, where a "Big-Bang Integration" caused a missed deadline by merging all components at once instead of gradually. Unfortunately, since "developers struggle to know if what they are doing makes sense for anyone else" [7], such a single integration step often leads to unexpected severe consequences.

The project consists of developing a real-time analytics system using edge computing, where researchers and industry professionals work as distributed teams on different components. An architectural overview of the created system is depicted in Fig. 1: two producers of data form the input of a real-time system, which analyses the data and produces the output for two consumers. They were developed by five different project partners.

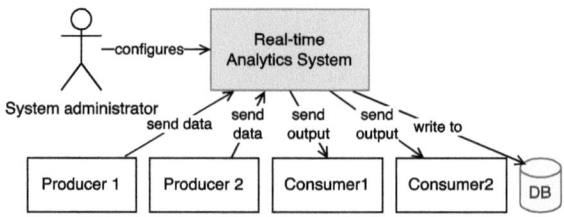

Fig. 1. Architecture (using the notation of a C4-model context diagram [4])

The described system poses significant challenges as it is a reactive system [3], processing sensor data in real time and forwarding the output to consumers. The database shown in Fig. 1 acts as a backup for incoming data in case the analytics subsystem fails. Producers are software components that generate data from sensors or other sources. Consumers, on the other hand, are components that use data generated either internally or from external sources. From the client's perspective, such systems are binary: they either work or they don't. For example, if the system processes the data correctly but fails to deliver the output to consumer two, it is still perceived as a failure.

The integration took place in two days at a location were the system could be tested. The idea was to do a first test one the day before the deadline and to make the final adjustments so that at the deadline the final product could be demonstrated. Already during the first day, we encountered several issues, e.g.: some hardware was initially not present and had to be retrieved; the network on the testing site was much slower than expected, this required the team to modify the source code on the first day to send data with a lower resolution; components had performance issues not encountered when developing them at the company sites; an important team member did not attend the integration, which transform in spend time to solve som issue.

2 Observations and Insights

In this project every project partner—naturally—developed its solution bottom-up. Following the GQM approach, we formulated the following questions:

Q1. *What were the issues with the integration?*

Q2. *Why did the team decide to build the software using a bottom-up approach?*

Q3. *Were there any early warning signs indicating that the deadline might not be met?*

We observed various challenges (answer to Q1): 1) research projects often require not only time for development but also time to discover what is yet not unknown; 2) collaboration across geographically dispersed teams from different organisations made it complex to expose problems; 3) it was complicated and expensive to test the entire system with all its parts, since expensive equipment and distributed team; 4) only team leads had weekly meetings, sometimes resulting in "Chinese whispers" among researchers; 5) developing systems in real-time processing, particularly within the framework of a reactive application, require the attention to details. Considering the fact that all resources are limited, the question is how to achieve the project goals with the given resources minimising the risk.

Agile methodologies often promote iterative development and early integration [11]. We understand this as promoting a "top-down" development approach in which one begins deploying a system that instead of real, functioning components just contains mock components, i.e., components that imitate the final ones. This would mean that the first deployed system should have been as the one in Fig. 1, where producers and consumers are either doing nothing or producing test data. As components are developed, mock components are replaced with implemented counterparts, which however, is not a "minimal viable product" (MVP) as nothing functions. It represents just the deployment of the architecture, so that one can test newly developed features immediately in a production-like environment.

Studying why the team chose to pursue a bottom-up approach (answer to Q2), we observed that producing test data was extremely difficult. Let's assume, one wants to build a face recognition door lock system, which cannot be circumvented using a photograph, one that uses 3D cameras. To test such a system I need to test it with real humans or obtain or create a testing dataset and use that as a testing input for the developed door lock system. In our case, such a data set did not exist, could not be easily created and manual testing was expensive. This leads to the first insight: **In projects where integration testing is difficult, we will dedicate time and foresee it in the project plan to create testing data to setup a mock architecture as soon as possible.**

In many projects involving machine learning and AI (as the present one), the development of the individual components can be very complex and require specialized researchers in particular areas. This leads to the second insight: **in projects where distributed components must work together to deliver the project's output, we will dedicate as much attention and resources to the communication infrastructure as we do to the components themselves.**

To further analyze Q2, we conducted a web search on Google on December 16th, 2024. The search was performed in incognito mode using the query "software engineering top-up top-down", and we reviewed the results from the first two pages. From this analysis Top-down approaches focus on planning and system-wide understanding [5] before implementation but can be inflexible and require more upfront resources [9]. They involve less communication between modules [10] and may struggle with unknowns at the start [5,10]. Bottom-up approaches prioritize coding and early testing, making them ideal for rapid prototyping [2,6]. However, they risk poor integration if modules are developed without a clear linking strategy. Bottom-up is favored for its focus on fundamentals before addressing the whole system [1].

These results suggest practitioners hesitate to view the system as a whole, which is key for early integration. The statements analysed above imply that top-down thinking requires full system understanding or works only with minimal module communication. We strongly disagree with these views.

This brief web search aligned with our project experience: the belief that the system could not yet be fully defined led to a bottom-up approach. There might also be psychological factors playing a role, including: a) it seems more productive to "fully develop" components rather than creating mock components, and b) it is more rewarding to build something that works than to create a component that is incomplete but uncovers communication issues with other components. This last point, uncovering communication problems, requires an open error culture within the team; otherwise, the issue is merely attributed to the component being "incomplete."

This brings us to the third insight: **in projects where distributed components must work together to deliver the project's output, we have to establish a top-down mindset within the team so that all know why it is worth to a) investing in building mock components and b) performing integration testing as early as possible.**

To answer Q3 (if there were early warning signs), we list the warning signs we observed during the project:

1) Procrastination in decision-making: Delays in reaching agreements on standards or resolving specific issues often led to bottlenecks. E.g. critical decisions were postponed until late in the project timeline.

2) Overemphasis on individual solutions: Many participants focused predominantly on optimising their own components rather than considering the system as an integrated whole.

3) Lack of shared prototypes for testing: Teams often failed to provide others with working prototypes or sample data necessary for testing.

4) Insufficient feedback mechanisms: The absence of robust communication and feedback systems between partners led to misalignment.

5) Operating too close to technological limits: The system frequently operated near the threshold. E.g. bandwidth utilization of 9.6 GB out of a 10 GB limit and server CPUs running at over 90% capacity.

6) Last-minute changes after integrated testing: As a consequence of the last-day integrated test, some parameters were changed overnight, forcing other partners to adapt without sufficient time for testing.

3 Conclusions

This experience report described our observations and insights of the development of a distributed reactive real-time system involving hardware and software.

Our key observation is that, although Agile methodologies promote early integration and continuous testing, their effective implementation remains challenging in multi-partner, distributed projects. For instance, while collaboration tools and regular cross-team meetings seem to solve distributed team challenges easily, in projects like ours with multiple partners, each has established ways of working and may resist changing their approach solely for the sake of one project. Similarly, while continuous integration and automated testing address minimal early testing, in our case, some teams implemented these practices independently without a unified, coordinated plan.

We Interpreted Those Findings Using Root Cause Analysis. Beyond technical difficulties, the primary drivers of the integration challenges were psychological factors such as a preference for 'finished' components over mock-ups, a lack of shared ownership of system-level risks, and communication barriers across organisational boundaries.

We want to prioritize the lessons learned as follows: first, unified communication infrastructure must be prioritized from the start, on par with technical development; second mock-based early deployment of the system architecture is critical, even if real components are not ready, and third, top-down thinking (intended as seeing the system as a whole rather than isolated parts) must be actively promoted within teams. Finally a better understanding and awareness of software management techniques specifically tailored for reactive projects can help reduce development risks.

Proposed Practices for Future Projects. To address these issues, we propose multiple action as: establish a shared simulation-driven integration environment from project inception, —even with only mock components—; one team as responsible of cross-integration demos and explicit resources and planning time to the creation of realistic test data and mock environments early in the project. Moreover, we suggest that adopting practices such as simulation-driven engineering [8] can lead to better outcomes and faster delivery timelines. When possible, managers and developers should favor the use of effective tools and development techniques over simply adding more meetings or resources, as this can lead to more efficient and successful project execution.

Open Questions for Further Research

1) How can effective collaboration be ensured between teams with differing goals? While coordination within a company or between aligned partners is straightforward, collaboration becomes more difficult when partners have diverging interests or incentives.

2) Can integration testing mitigate the effects of weak organisational alignment? Even if not all stakeholders share the same goals, can a robust integration testing strategy ensure coherence and project success?

3) Can specific tools or frameworks better support these projects? Would shifting from high-level planning to practical tooling help managers and developers stay goal-oriented and reduce unnecessary methodological overhead?

4) What is the optimal trade-off between planning and execution? Meetings and formal coordination consume resources. How much planning is truly necessary to avoid inefficiency without losing critical alignment?

These open questions point toward a broader research agenda: evaluating how structured practices–such as mandatory cross-partner mock-based integration, simulation-driven environments, and lightweight tooling–can systematically improve coordination and resilience in reactive, distributed systems. Empirical studies or controlled experiments comparing these practices across similar project contexts could provide deeper insights and lead to evidence-based guidelines.

Implications for Future Development Methodologies. We suggest that current software development practices–particularly Agile–should be adapted to better support the unique challenges of reactive, distributed systems, especially in multi-partner environments. Reactive systems and collaborative projects introduce complexities that often exceed the capabilities of traditional project management techniques, increasing the risk of failure, particularly during large-scale integrations. Enhancing awareness of software management strategies tailored for reactive development, incorporating warning signals to prompt timely adjustments, and adopting approaches such as simulation-driven engineering [8] and lightweight, mandatory cross-partner integration cycles may reduce development risks, improve delivery timelines, and lead to more successful project outcomes.

References

1. Andrea Griffini: Is is preferable to design top down or bottom up?. https://softwareengineering.stackexchange.com/questions/134633/is-is-preferable-to-design-top-down-or-bottom-up
2. Ashborne: Top-down and Bottom-up Approach: The Difference in Software Engineering (2024). https://medium.com/@ashbornee/top-down-and-bottom-up-approach-the-difference-in-software-engineering-c6c159389a00
3. Bonér, J., Farley, D., Kuhn, R., Thompson, M.: The Reactive Manifesto (2014). https://www.reactivemanifesto.org. Accessed 24 Jan 2025
4. Brown, S.: The C4 model for visualising software architecture. LeanPub (2023)
5. Dzikri Qalam: Software Engineering Strategy: Top-Down Approach (2024). https://dzikriqalam.medium.com/software-engineering-strategy-top-down-approach-0ae010214d54
6. Kushleen Waraich: Difference Between Top Down and Bottom up Approach (2024), https://www.naukri.com/code360/library/difference-between-top-down-and-bottom-up-approach
7. Mellegard, N., Burden, H., Levin, D., Lind, K., Magazinius, A.: Contrasting big bang with continuous integration through defect reports. IEEE Softw. **37**(3) (2020)
8. Meyers, J.: Simulation-driven design: A closer look at how engineers can save time, resources, and manpower by frontloading simulation - Industrial Machinery (2024). https://blogs.sw.siemens.com/industrial-machinery/2024/10/08/simulation-driven-design-a-closer-look-at-frontloading-simulation/
9. No author: Top Down Approach in Software Engineering. https://prepinsta.com/software-engineering/top-down-approach/

10. No author: Difference between Bottom-Up Model and Top-Down Model (2022). https://www.geeksforgeeks.org/difference-between-bottom-up-model-and-top-down-model/
11. Pasuksmit, J., Thongtanunam, P., Karunasekera, S.: A systematic literature review on reasons and approaches for accurate effort estimations in agile. ACM Comput. Surv. **56**(11) (2024)

Open Access This chapter is licensed under the terms of the Creative Commons Attribution 4.0 International License (http://creativecommons.org/licenses/by/4.0/), which permits use, sharing, adaptation, distribution and reproduction in any medium or format, as long as you give appropriate credit to the original author(s) and the source, provide a link to the Creative Commons license and indicate if changes were made.

The images or other third party material in this chapter are included in the chapter's Creative Commons license, unless indicated otherwise in a credit line to the material. If material is not included in the chapter's Creative Commons license and your intended use is not permitted by statutory regulation or exceeds the permitted use, you will need to obtain permission directly from the copyright holder.

Novice Programmers' Experiences with Hybrid vs. In-Person Pair Programming – A Comparative Study

Mary Giblin(✉) and Sheila Fallon

Department of Computer and Software Engineering, Technological University of the Shannon, Athlone, Co. Westmeath, Ireland
{Mary.Giblin,Sheila.Fallon}@tus.ie

Abstract. Pair programming is a well-established practice in agile software development which is used to improve software quality and enhance learning and knowledge sharing. Agile proponents emphasise face-to-face interaction as a fundamental principle of agile teams. However, in today's hybrid work environment, organisations and teams are increasingly adapting Agile practices to incorporate remote and hybrid collaboration. This study explores the experiences of novice programmers engaging in both remote or hybrid and in-person pair programming, analysing programming session length and role switching, satisfaction levels and challenges, as well as impact of the environment and recommendations for improvement. Practitioners conducted some pairing sessions face-to-face and some sessions remotely. We found that hybrid/remote pair programming sessions included more breaks but showed less frequent role switching and lower satisfaction levels compared to face-to-face settings, highlighting a need for better tools and practices to support remote collaboration.

Keyword: Pair Programming · Hybrid Work · Collaboration · Practices

1 Introduction

Pair programming is a core practice in Agile software development and Extreme Programming (XP). In a typical session, two developers collaborate at a single computer, each assuming distinct roles. One acts as the **driver**, actively writing the code, while the other, the **navigator**, carefully reviews it, suggests improvements, and anticipates future challenges [1]. This dynamic encourages real-time feedback, enhances code quality, and fosters collaborative problem-solving [2]. Pair programming emerged as a co-located practice, with dedicated workstations available to support seamless collaboration between pairs [3].

Several studies, including [4, 5] and [6], have examined the impact of pair programming. Since the outbreak Covid-19, numerous studies have explored the effects of remote working on software development and productivity. Ralph et al. [7] found that remote working could negatively impact productivity, while Smite et al. [8] observed that perceived productivity remained largely unchanged. However, they also noted a variability, with some developers (working remotely) reporting increased productivity while others experienced a decline.

The goal of this study is to compare the experiences of novice programmers as they engage in both hybrid remote and face-to-face pair programming. By having the same participants experience both modes, this study aims to analyse differences in collaboration dynamics (e.g. length of pairing sessions, role switching) as well as technical challenges and overall satisfaction. We seek to answer the following research questions:

1. *How do novice programmers' experiences with pair programming differ between hybrid/remote and face-to-face environments?*
2. *How do novice programmers' experiences with pair programming in hybrid/remote and face-to-face environments compare to those programmers with mixed experience levels, as reported in the existing literature?*

The research aims to provide insights into how hybrid/remote and face-to-face programming impacts novice programmers and inform best practices for integrating novice programmers effectively into hybrid software development teams. This paper contains some preliminary findings.

2 Background and Related Work

In a hybrid scenario, communication gaps often emerge. Remote participants lack the benefit of in-person cues like body language, which can lead to misunderstandings. Lack of clarity can hamper progress especially when non-verbal cues are missing [10]. Digital communication tools have limitations – poor network quality or audio/video lag can reduce communication quality, with tone and emotion often lost or misunderstood over calls [11].

A notable challenge in hybrid pair programming is ensuring both partners remain equally engaged. When one developer is in the office (potentially with access to large screens tor face-to-face support from others) and the other is remote (potentially feeling isolated), imbalances in engagement can arise. Over time, the remote member may become more passive, turning into a "silent observer" rather than an active navigator. Research confirms that a mixed-mode pairing (one on-site, one remote) is often the least effective configuration [12]. In a recent case study at a fintech company, developers paired in various modes (fully on-site, fully remote, and mixed) reported that the mixed sessions were the least advantageous in terms of collaboration and outcomes [12]. This suggests that the remote partner in a hybrid pair may not get the same level of involvement as they would if both were co-located or both remote.

3 Methodology

This research employed a qualitative and comparative design involving 25 participants enrolled in a graduate internship program as part of their Master's degree in Software Engineering. These interns had come from undergraduate courses in computing and engineering disciplines. As part of the Masters they completed modules specifically covering Agile methodologies, including Scrum, Extreme Programming (XP), and pair programming. Additionally, they had completed coursework in Object-Oriented Programming using Java, Database Architecture and Cloud Computing, equipping them with the technical proficiency required for the programming tasks involved.

As part of the study, participants were asked to perform pair programming tasks in two different settings: first, face-to-face (both participants physically present), and second, a hybrid scenario (one participant remote and the other physically present). These tasks were based directly on user stories and practical software development activities provided by the industry partner.

The research objective is framed by the following two questions:

1. *How do novice programmers' experiences with pair programming differ between hybrid/remote and face-to-face environments?*
2. *How do novice programmers' experiences with pair programming in hybrid/remote and face-to-face environments compare to those programmers with mixed experience levels, as reported in the existing literature?*

4 Initial Results

4.1 Session Management and Participant Satisfaction in Programming Tasks

Table 1. Number of Sessions to Complete Programming Task by Mode

Number of Sessions	Face-to-Face(%)	Hybrid/Remote(%)
1–2	56%	60%
3–5	44%	40%
>5	0%	0%

Table 2. Average Length of Pair Programming Sessions

Average Length of Sessions	Face-to-Face(%)	Hybrid/Remote(%)
<30 min	12%	8%
30–60 min	76%	60%
60–120 min	12%	32%

Table 3. Occurrence of Breaks During Pair Programming Sessions

Take a break	Face-to-Face(%)	Hybrid/Remote(%)
Yes	42%	56%
No	58%	44%

Table 4. Switching of Roles During a Single Pairing Session

Switching of roles	Face-to-Face(%)	Hybrid/Remote(%)
Yes	65%	50%
No	35%	50%

Table 5. Switching of Roles over Multiple Pairing Session

Switching of roles	Face-to-Face(%)	Hybrid/Remote(%)
Yes	88%	68%
No	12%	32%

Table 6. Overall Satisfaction with Pair Programming Experiences

Satisfaction Level	Face-to-Face(%)	Hybrid/Remote(%)
Very Satisfied	50%	36%
Somewhat Satisfied	46%	56%
Neutral	4%	8%

5 Preliminary Findings and Future Work

5.1 Task Completion and Session Duration

As shown in Table 1, the majority of participants in both face-to-face (56%) and hybrid/remote (60%) settings completed the task within 1–2 sessions. This suggests broadly comparable efficiency across modalities.

However, session duration varied notably between the two modes (Table 2). In face-to-face settings, 76% of sessions lasted between 30 and 60 min. In contrast, hybrid/remote sessions were more likely to be longer, with 32% lasting 60–120 min and 60% falling into the 30 to 60-min range. This indicates that, while number of programming sessions were similar, remote sessions tended to be longer.

5.2 Breaks and Role Switching

Hybrid/remote sessions were more likely to incorporate breaks (56%) compared to face-to-face sessions (42%), suggesting a potential need for more intentional rest periods when collaborating remotely (Table 3). Differences were also observed in role-switching behaviors. During single pairing sessions, 65% of face-to-face participants reported switching roles completed to 50% in hybrid/remote settings (Table 4). Over multiple sessions, the difference was more pronounced: 88% of face-to-face participants reported switching roles compared to 68% in hybrid/remote sessions (Table 5). This is consistent with research emphasising fluidity and ease of interaction in co-located pair programming sessions [9]. This is also supported by the following quotation from the qualitative data. *"Despite its benefits, remote PP presents challenges such as slower role-switching and limited code highlighting by the navigator. We propose leveraging new technologies like Cloud or Collaborative IDEs to mitigate these issues and enable equal participation between members and dynamic role-switching."*

5.3 Participant Satisfaction

As shown in Table 6, satisfaction with pair programming was higher in face-to-face sessions (50% reporting being "very satisfied") than in hybrid/remote sessions (36%). This finding is consistent with prior studies underscoring the importance of direct, face-to-face communication and social interaction for participant satisfaction in pair programming [12]. Moving forward, this research will collect more data and explore the factors influencing lower satisfaction levels in hybrid and remote contexts by analysing the qualitative data. Further studies should tailor the questions to investigate effective strategies to optimise remote pair programming practices, including the role of technology, session structuring, and team dynamics.

Acknowledgments. This study was partly funded by the N-TUTORR National Programme and SATLE (Strategic Alignment of Teaching and Learning Enhancement Funding in Higher Education.

Disclosure of Interests. Authors have no competing interests.

References

1. Williams, L., Kessler, R.R.: Pair programming illuminated. Addison-Wesley Professional (2003)
2. Laplante, P.A.: "Pair Programming" in Encyclopedia of Software Engineering Three-Volume Set (Print), Auerbach Publications (2010)
3. Robinson, H., Sharp, H.: Organisational culture and XP: three case studies. In: Proceedings of Agile Development Conference (ADC 2005), pp. 49–58. IEEE (2005)
4. Man Lui, K., Chan, K.C.C.: pair programming productivity: novice-novice vs. Expert-Expert. Int. J. Hum.-Comput. Stud. **64**(9), 915–925 (2006)
5. Vanhanen, J., Korpi, H.: Experiences of using pair programming in an agile project. 40th Annual Hawaii International Conference System Sciences 2007. HICSS 2007, pp. 274b–274b (2007)

6. Han, K.W., Lee, E., Lee, Y.: The impact of a peer-learning agent based on pair programming in a programming course. IEEE Trans. Educ. **53**(2), 318–327 (2010)
7. Ralph, P., et al.: Pandemic programming. Empir. Softw. Eng. **25**(6), 4927–4961 (2020)
8. Smite, D., Tkalich, A., Moe, N.B., Papatheocharous, E., Klotins, E., Buvik, M.P.: Changes in perceived productivity of software engineers during COVID-19 pandemic: the voice of evidence. J. Syst. Softw. **186**, 111197 (2022)
9. Conboy, K., Moe, N.B., Stray, V., Gundelsby, J.H.: The future of hybrid software development: challenging current assumptions. IEEE Softw. **40**(02), 26–33 (2023). https://doi.org/10.1109/MS.2022.3230449
10. Tech Journey. https://techjourney.it-jobs.de/en/it-skills/pair-program-tandem-programming-as-a-working-technique-in-software-development. Accessed 8 March 2025
11. Smite, D., Mikalsen, M., Moe, N.B., Stray, V., Klotins, E.: From collaboration to solitude and back: remote pair programming during COVID-19. In: Gregory, P., de Souza, R.K.B., Petruccioli, A. (eds.) Agile Processes in Software Engineering and Extreme Programming, pp. 3–18. Springer (2021)
12. Tkalich, A., Moe, N.B., Andersen, N.H., Stray, V., Barbala, A.M.: Pair programming practiced in hybrid work (2023)

Open Access This chapter is licensed under the terms of the Creative Commons Attribution 4.0 International License (http://creativecommons.org/licenses/by/4.0/), which permits use, sharing, adaptation, distribution and reproduction in any medium or format, as long as you give appropriate credit to the original author(s) and the source, provide a link to the Creative Commons license and indicate if changes were made.

The images or other third party material in this chapter are included in the chapter's Creative Commons license, unless indicated otherwise in a credit line to the material. If material is not included in the chapter's Creative Commons license and your intended use is not permitted by statutory regulation or exceeds the permitted use, you will need to obtain permission directly from the copyright holder.

Rethink Agile Scaling with Robotics Subsumption Architecture

Sue Ryu(✉)

Aha Autonomy, LLC, Woodland Park, NJ, USA
Sue.Ryu@AhaAutonomy.com

Abstract. Agile fosters speed, autonomy, and innovation at the team level, but organizations often struggle to preserve these strengths as they scale. Coordination overhead increases, decision-making slows, and the agility that once fueled success begins to erode. This paper introduces an approach to scaling by drawing on **Robotics Subsumption Architecture**, a model originally developed to build adaptive, autonomous robots. Building on the late **Mike Beedle**'s pioneering work in applying these robotics principles to organization design**,** we reimagine how to design systems that grow without sacrificing local autonomy or real-time responsiveness. This approach offers scalable agility by embedding sensing, decision-making, and action into every layer—resulting in organizations that are resilient, decentralized, and capable of surviving today's VUCA market.

Keywords: Agile Scaling · Business Agility · Enterprise Scrum · Subsumption Architecture

1 Introduction

Agile has transformed how organizations deliver value by enabling speed, autonomy, and innovation at the team level. However, as organizations scale Agile across teams, coordination challenges and slower decision-making often erode the very autonomy that made it successful. How can organizations grow while preserving the agility that helped them thrive?

In this paper, we explore an approach inspired by robotics: the Subsumption Architecture. Building on the late Mike Beedle's pioneering work in applying its principles to organization design, we reimagine how to build organizations that are resilient, decentralized, and capable of dynamic, real-time adaptation—even as they scale.

2 Background

2.1 Robotics Subsumption Architecture

Developed by Prof. Rodney Brooks in the 1980s, **Subsumption Architecture** introduced a revolutionary **architecture** for building intelligent, adaptive systems. It was proposed in opposition to traditional **symbolic AI**, which attempted to guide behavior through internal models and symbolic mental representations of the world. It does this by decomposing the complete behavior into sub-behaviors. These sub-behaviors are organized into a hierarchy of layers. Each layer implements a particular level of behavioral competence, and higher levels are able to subsume lower levels (= integrate/combine lower levels to a more comprehensive whole) in order to create viable behavior. For example, a robot's lowest layer could be "Avoid Objects." The second layer would be "Wander Around," which runs beneath the third layer "Explore World." Because a robot must have the ability to "Avoid Objects" in order to "Wander Around" effectively, the Subsumption Architecture creates a system in which the higher layers utilize the lower-level competencies. The layers, which all receive sensor information, work in parallel and generate outputs. These outputs can be commands to actuators, or signals that suppress or inhibit other layers [1].

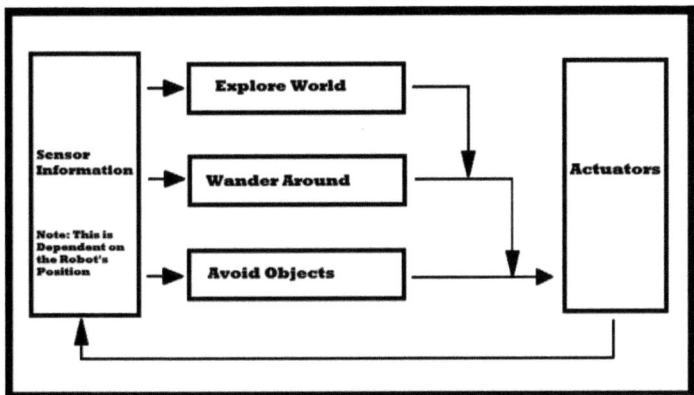

Fig. 1. Abstract representation of subsumption architecture, with the higher layers subsuming the roles of lower layers when the sensory information determines it. [1]

As shown in Fig. 1, **three core functions** are

- **Subsumption Layers**: The behavior of exploring the world is divided into three hierarchical layers: Avoid Objects (lowest layer), Wander Around (middle layer), Explore World (highest layer). Higher layers subsume lower layers, meaning they can override their functions when necessary to achieve more complex behavior.
- **Sensor**: Continuously monitors the environment and feeds real-time signals to all layers simultaneously.
- **Actuators**: Execute actions based on which layers have been activated, ensuring appropriate responses to the environment.

It is this continuous interaction among these three functions—where layers react to sensor signals and trigger actuators based on defined conditions—that allows the system to behave in real time, without requiring centralized control or symbolic reasoning. As the robot moves through its environment, it continuously collects and integrates data from past interactions to adjust its behavior on the fly, identifying more effective paths and responses based on what it has encountered. Before Subsumption Architecture, robotics research pursued centralized intelligent systems that modeled the environment internally and attempted high-level strategic decision-making. However, these systems failed to perform reliably in dynamic, real-world environments. The complexity overwhelmed centralized models, and successes were limited to highly constrained tasks, such as developing a smart chess game. Recognizing this failure, Prof. Rodney Brooks proposed a radical new approach: abandon complex internal models and focus on real-time environmental interaction through layered, autonomous behaviors. This breakthrough fundamentally changed the trajectory of robotics and adaptive systems design.

2.2 Comparison with Established Agile Scaling Frameworks

While frameworks like SAFe, LeSS, and Scrum@Scale aim to bring order and coordination to scaling Agile, they often rely on structured, top-down mechanisms that can hinder adaptability and autonomy. In contrast, Robotics Subsumption Architecture provides a fundamentally different paradigm for scaling Agile. Just as it revolutionized robotics, this architecture has the potential to do the same for Agile scaling. Rather than building hierarchy to manage complexity, subsumption-based ecosystems distribute sensing and action across layers, allowing the system to continuously adjust and evolve.

3 Agile Scaling Through Subsumption

3.1 Building Blocks of Customer-Focused Organization

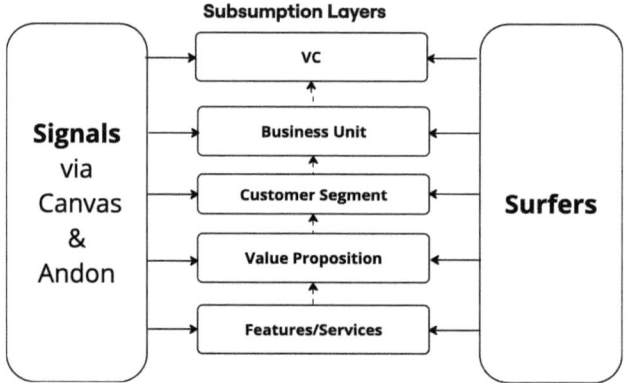

Fig. 2. Illustrating how Subsumption principles are applied to customer focused org. ecosystem.

- **Subsumption Layers**: The organization uses customer segments as the base to build its subsumption layers, resulting in five hierarchical levels: VC (top layer), Business Unit (2nd), Customer Segment (3rd), Value Proposition (4th), and Features/Services (bottom layer). Higher layers subsume lower layers, ensuring strategic alignment while preserving autonomy at its own layer.

- **Signals via Canvas & Andon**: Just as sensors provide real time data in robotics, business canvases and Andon-style signaling systems facilitate real-time information sharing and decision-making across layers.
- **Surfers:** Surfers move fluidly across layers, guiding decisions and optimizing workflows. Surfers are domain experts who move fluidly across teams and layers. They gather real-time information, assess emerging conditions, and coordinate actions across the organization. Surfers enable decentralized yet synchronized decision-making without relying on hierarchical command structures.
- **No Central Control**: Instead of relying on top-down control, Signals, Layers, and Surfers work together to maintain alignment and responsiveness at scale.

By embracing this model, organizations can embed agility throughout the entire system, ensuring speed, autonomy, and resilience in scaling (Fig. 2).

3.2 Applying the Model: eAuction

eAuction is a dynamic digital auction platform designed to serve multiple industries, beginning with airline ticket auctions and later expanding into entertainment, sports, and fine arts. As eAuction grew rapidly, the company needed an organizational ecosystem that could scale while preserving the speed and autonomy that made its early success possible. To achieve this, eAuction applied principles of Robotics Subsumption Architecture to its organizational ecosystem. Rather than relying on centralized management, the company structured itself into layered, autonomous teams capable of responding to real-time conditions such as *market changes, customer needs, or internal tensions*.

Startup Phase: Building from the Bottom-Up Approach
In its startup phase, eAuction adopted a bottom-up approach to building its business, beginning with services tailored for the airline industry. The Fig. 3 below illustrates how Subsumption Architecture was first applied:

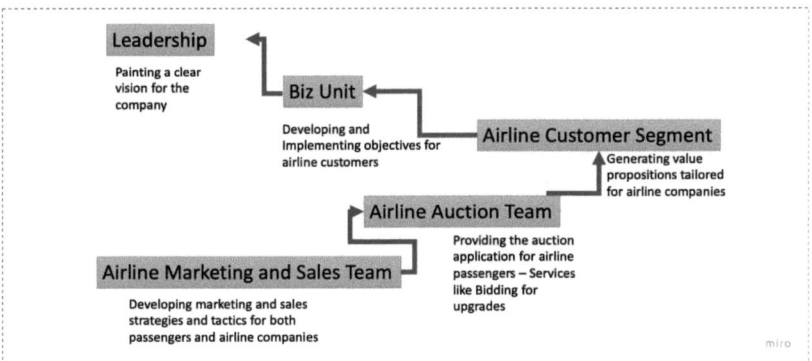

Fig. 3. eAuction's bottom-up approach of applying the subsumption architecture at the start-up stage.

Starting with the Airline Marketing and Sales Team - developing marketing strategies and tactics for both passengers and airline companies, the organization layered upward through specialized teams: the Airline Auction team (responsible for services like bidding apps for ticket upgrades), the Airline Customer Segment team (focus on generating a portfolio of value propositions for the airline customers), and the Business Unit team (developing and implementing objectivities for airline customers). All of this was anchored by Leadership team, which painted a clear vision for the company. This bottom-up evolution exemplifies how autonomy and responsiveness were preserved while building toward strategic alignment.

Expansion Phase: Diversification and Structural Adaptation

eAuction has evolved from an airline auction platform into a dynamic, multi-segment marketplace. Today, it serves four key customer segments: Airline Companies, Music Stars, Sports Leagues, and Artists. By structuring operations around customer segments, eAuction expands seamlessly while maintaining autonomy and adaptability.

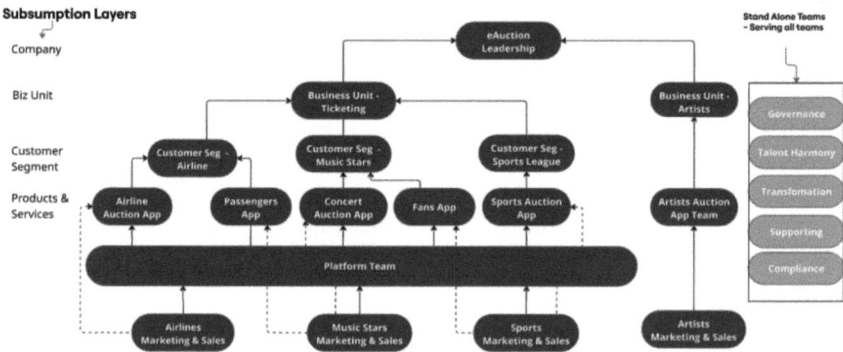

Fig. 4. Snapshot of eAuction's Organization structure at the current stage of their growth.

Figure 4 illustrates how eAuction used customer segments as the base to build its subsumption layers. The four layers—Company/Leadership (top), Business Units (2nd), Customer Segments (3rd), and Products & Services (bottom)—reflect a structure grounded in customer needs. This foundation enabled eAuction to diversify while preserving focus and autonomy. The figure highlights the resulting diversified customer segment teams, a spun-off Business Unit dedicated to Artists, a centralized Platform Team for ticketing, and standalone service teams—such as Governance, Talent Harmony, Transformation, Supporting, and Compliance—that provide organization-wide support. Notably, eAuction spun off a distinct Artists Business Unit to serve the unique needs of creators who auction artwork rather than sell event tickets. This structural separation allowed for tailored value propositions, marketing, and applications—while preserving responsiveness through the subsumption model.

One important structural detail is the presence of a **Platform Team** that serves all auction-related product teams under the Business Unit - Ticketing. This includes the apps supporting airlines, passengers, music stars, music fans, sport leagues, and sports fans. However, the Platform Team does **not** serve the Artists Auction App team, as the nature of that business differs significantly—artists do not sell tickets but rather artworks, requiring separate tooling and workflow. Additionally, eAuction introduced a set of **stand-alone service teams—Governance, Talent Harmony, Transformation, Supporting, and Compliance**. These units operate outside of the subsumption layers and provide essential, shared capabilities across the entire organization. While they are not embedded within the business units directly, they enable the whole organization to function effectively and responsibly at scale.

The current organizational ecosystem for eAuction works through the integration of Subsumption Layers, Canvases, Surfers, and Signals—a triad that forms the foundation of its decentralized organization ecosystem. These elements don't operate in isolation; rather, it is the way they are glued together that enables the organization to function as a cohesive, adaptive whole. Surfers fluidly connect efforts across teams, and Signals and canvases provide constant real-time awareness. These mechanisms allow decentralized teams to respond rapidly and coherently without requiring central command. What we see in Fig. 4 is a snapshot of eAuction's growth—a moment in time. As the company continues to expand, pivot, or respond to shifting market demands, their organization ecosystem is expected to evolve. For an organization to remain fast and agile, all components— teams, signals, surfers, and shared services—must work in concert to continuously adapt and align to emerging conditions.

4 Outcomes and Benefits

The application of Subsumption Architecture to Agile organizations has produced a number of tangible outcomes:

- **Autonomy at the Core**: Teams operate independently and make decisions locally without waiting for approvals—yet higher layers retain the ability to override when necessary to maintain strategic alignment.
- **Decentralized Decision-Making**: Subsumption layers promote decentralized control, dramatically reducing the friction and delays caused by traditional command-and-control hierarchies.
- **Happier Teams, Customers, and Stakeholders:** It fosters self-management, leading to more engaged teams, improved customer outcomes, and ultimately, satisfied stakeholders.
- **Survival and Profitability:** In today's complex and volatile markets, adaptability is essential. Subsumption Architecture enables organizations to respond rapidly to change—improving both resilience and profitability.

Reference

1. Brooks, R.: The early history of the new AI. Cambrian Intell. **8–12**, 15–16 (1999)

Open Access This chapter is licensed under the terms of the Creative Commons Attribution 4.0 International License (http://creativecommons.org/licenses/by/4.0/), which permits use, sharing, adaptation, distribution and reproduction in any medium or format, as long as you give appropriate credit to the original author(s) and the source, provide a link to the Creative Commons license and indicate if changes were made.

The images or other third party material in this chapter are included in the chapter's Creative Commons license, unless indicated otherwise in a credit line to the material. If material is not included in the chapter's Creative Commons license and your intended use is not permitted by statutory regulation or exceeds the permitted use, you will need to obtain permission directly from the copyright holder.

Author Index

A
Abrahamsson, Pekka 3
Adil, Mahum 32
Aneggi, Alessandro 101
Aranda, Gabriela 68

B
Broomandi, Fateme 53

C
Christensen, Emily Laue 53

F
Fallon, Sheila 108

G
Garcés, Kelly 68
García, Félix O. 68
Giblin, Mary 108

H
Hanssen, Geir K. 3
Hasan, Md Toufique 22
Herda, Tomas 3
Hyrynsalmi, Sonja 53

J
Janes, Andrea 101

K
Kemell, Kai-Kristian 22
Khan, Ayman Asad 22
Khanna, Dron 53
Kwok, Ya Ting Crystal 32

L
Leybourn, Evan 14

M
Masood, Zainab 78
Morales, Christopher 14

N
Neumann, Michael 91

P
Paasivaara, Maria 53
Pichler, Victoria 3
Planötscher, Daniel 41

R
Rasku, Jussi 22
Rauschenberger, Maria 91
Rolón, Elvira 68
Ryu, Sue 114

S
Saari, Mika 22
Schön, Eva-Maria 91
Senapathi, Mali 91
Silva da Silva, Tiago 91
Soto, Juan Pablo 68

T
Tyagi, Sulabh 78

V
Vizcaíno, Aurora 68

Z
Zhang, Zheying 3

MIX
Papier aus verantwortungsvollen Quellen
Paper from responsible sources
FSC® C105338

If you have any concerns about our products,
you can contact us on
ProductSafety@springernature.com

In case Publisher is established outside the EU,
the EU authorized representative is:
**Springer Nature Customer Service Center GmbH
Europaplatz 3, 69115 Heidelberg, Germany**

Printed by Libri Plureos GmbH
in Hamburg, Germany